MW00450484

## Disclaimer & Copyright

must consult your doctor or get professional medical advice before using any of the suggested remedies, techniques, or information in this book.

Upon using the information contained in this book, you agree to hold harmless the Author from and against any damages, costs, and expenses, including any legal fees potentially resulting from the application of any of the information provided by this guide. This disclaimer applies to any damages or injury caused by the use and application, whether directly or indirectly, of any advice or information presented, whether for breach of contract, tort, negligence, personal injury, criminal intent, or under any other cause of action.

You agree to accept all risks of using the information presented inside this book. You need to consult a professional medical practitioner in order to ensure you are both able and healthy enough to participate in this program.

of the publisher, except in the case of brief quotations embodied in critical reviews and certain other noncommercial uses permitted by copyright law. For permission requests, contact the publisher, at the address below.

http://www.siimland.com.

Cover design by Siim Land.

# *Table of Contents*

Contents

# *Introduction*

## *An Utopian World Scenario*

Throughout history mankind has sought ways of taking care of the primary needs of any living organism – food and shelter. The hunter-gatherer lifestyle was uncertain and difficult, yet incredibly sustainable. Foraging shaped the physiology and psychology of our species.

After the adoption of agriculture, we managed to grow and store our own calories, which enabled us to do other activities that nourished the soul. Civilization flourished and spread across the globe. Now we're even reaching out to space.

But the aboriginal issue of eating still remains. Most of the world goes to bed hungry and nothing is certain. Science has created Genetically Modified Organisms (GMOs) to make superior food but at the moment we don't know what long term effects they might have on the body. Our current skill-level probably isn't up to par. There are also other concerns about health, ethics, sustainability and accessibility that all need to be taken into account.

Veganism includes those issues. It's a movement that is gaining a lot of popularity and has been a part of some human cultures for a long time. The core ideology is based on the premise that all sentient beings should be treated with respect, and that the consumption of animal products in any shape or form is unethical. Vegans eat a plant based diet, which tends to be high in carbohydrates.

On the other side, there are also ancestral Paleo movements that follow the opposite approach. Ketogenic low carb diets are high in fat and the majority of calories come from animal products, whether that be meat, eggs or butter. It has been successfully used for rapid weight loss, against diabetes, metabolic syndrome and other diseases. It's very healthy and an enjoyable way of eating.

But it's not the meat that makes a diet ketogenic. You wouldn't think that a vegan could sustainably eat low carb and stay in ketosis for the long term, but it's possible.

By picking up this book, chances are you're either a vegan wanting to try the ketogenic diet, someone who hasn't tried either of them, or someone who wants to know whether or not it's possible to stay keto while eating only plant based foods.

Whatever the case might be, you will definitely find this useful. Even if you don't follow a vegan approach, you can still benefit from reading this.

My name is Siim Land and I'm a holistic health practitioner, a fitness expert, a nutritionist and an author, among many other things. I've been doing the ketogenic diet for a very long time now and have managed to accumulate a wealth of knowledge on the subject.

For me, keto has been life transforming. I've managed to improve my health, performance both physical and mental, increased my longevity and energy. I'm not a vegan but thanks to my experience I can still help you start a ketogenic diet. It's a common problem that I get asked, to which I can give you a solution for.

In a utopian world scenario, we wouldn't have to kill anything. We would just be able to cover our physiological energy requirements by consuming some sort of magic pills full of calories and macronutrients. But we don't live in such a place, at least for the time being. The lion still hunts down the gazelle and man will still eat animals in the near future.

Nevertheless, a vegan ketogenic diet is an interesting experiment. Can the long term benefits of ketosis be achieved with only plant based foods? I guess we'll find out by the end of this book.

**Vegan Keto will help you:**

- Burn body fat, not muscle. Weight loss doesn't equal fat loss.
- Improve your mental focus and make your mind as sharp as a knife.
- Battle diabetes and potentially reverse it.
- Improve your health markers, such as blood pressure, blood sugar levels, cholesterol etc.
- Protect yourself against cancer, tumors and coronary heart disease.
- Increase your longevity and insulin sensitivity.
- Become fat adapted and start using fat for fuel.
- Experience mental clarity and feel amazing.
- Have access to abundant energy all the time.
- Reduce your hunger and lose sugar cravings for good.

- Eat mouthwatering and delicious meals that leave you satiated for long periods of time.

All while staying within the parameters of ketosis and veganism. It's probably the most innovative and complex diet plans out there. We don't have to lose our minds or conscience to eat a low carb plant based diet. If you want to try keto as a vegan, then this book is just for you.

# Chapter I

## Ketosis the Old Fashioned Way

This is a very niche specific book dedicated to a small but growing audience. At the same time, we can't expect to not go over some of the fundamentals. If you're a vegan, then you probably know only the outer layers of ketosis. No carbs, only meat, right? At first glance, it's just that, but there's also a lot more you need to know about.

Before we start a vegan ketogenic diet, we have to understand the principles of ketosis and this mysterious metabolic state. I'll keep it simple and could easily explain it to a child.

If you want to successfully follow a vegan keto diet, then you have to understand the principles of ketosis. Otherwise you would not be able to maintain it long term.

The human body is a complex system that can adapt to almost anything. It has found a solution to solving the bioenergetics component of being self-sufficient and resourceful. Ketosis is just that – an irreplaceable part of our biology that creates endogenous (from within) energy.

There are different fuel sources the body uses. When we're born, we get all of the energy we need from our mother's breast milk, at least that's what we did in the past, which puts us into ketosis. As we grow up, we begin to eat different foods, comprising of the 3 macronutrients: protein, carbs and fat. This primes our body to be using glucose, which is a carbohydrate molecule, and sets it as our primary default fuel source. There's nothing wrong with that, the thing is that in today's society most people have drifted too far away from their aboriginal ketogenic pathways, which causes obesity, diabetes and other ailments. Luckily, there is a way to circumvent that.

**In a nutshell, ketosis is a metabolic state in which the body has shifted from using glucose as the primary fuel source into supplying its energy demands with ketone bodies.** This happens when the liver glycogen stores are depleted and a substitute is necessary for the brain to maintain its functioning.

Both carbohydrates and fats can be used for the production of energy, but they're different in quality. However, in the presence of both, the body will always prefer the <u>former</u> because sugar can be easily accessed and quickly absorbed. To get the most out of the latter, there needs to be a period of keto-adaptation. The length of it depends on how reliant you are of glucose and how well your body accepts this new fuel source.

**Ketosis is an altered, but still natural, metabolic state that occurs either over a prolonged period of fasting or by restricting carbohydrate intake significantly, usually up to less than 50 grams per day** [i].

After an overnight fast already, our liver glycogen stores will be depleted and *Captain Liver* starts to produce more ketone bodies. This, in return, will increase the availability of fatty acids in the blood stream which the body then begins to utilize for the production of energy. It can be derived from both food and the adipose tissue.

This process is called beta-oxidation. When fat is broken down by the liver, glycerol and fatty acid molecules are released. The fatty acid gets broken down even more through ketogenesis that produces a ketone body called acetoacetate. This is then converted further into two other type of ketone bodies. (1)

Beta-hydroxybutyrate (BHB), which is the preferred fuel source for the brain and (2) acetone, that can be metabolized into glucose, but is mainly excreted as waste.

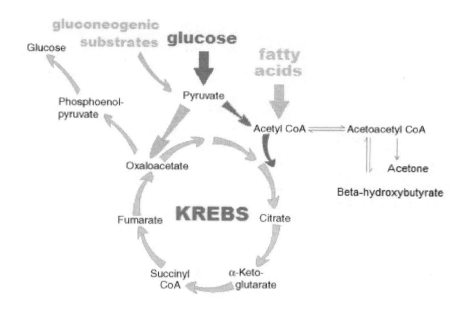

When you're running on glucose you go down the pathway of glycolysis and create pyruvate. All of these actions get burned inside the mitochondria and you can get <u>25% more energy from using beta-hydroxybutyrate</u> as fuel. In this scenario of fat utilization, we're taking the more efficient route that increases the density of our cellular power plants.

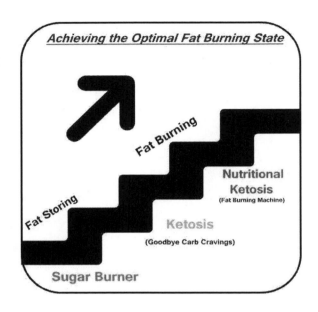

Nutritional ketosis is not the same as ketoacidosis, which causes the pH levels in the blood to drop and become acidic. This can result with a coma and eventually death. Usually, the body manages to maintain the acidity of the blood within a normal range despite the presence of ketones. Ketoacidosis occurs mostly with type-1 diabetes and excessive alcohol consumption.

After the initial period of adaptation, the body's biochemistry will be completely altered. Approximately 75% of the energy used by the brain will be provided by ketones and the liver will change its enzymes from dominantly digesting carbohydrates to actually preferring fat [ii]. Protein catabolism decreases significantly, as fat stores are mobilized and the use of ketones increases. Muscle glycogen gets used even less and the majority of our caloric demands will be derived from the adipose tissue.

Nutritional ketosis is perfectly safe and a great metabolic state to be in. This process is an adaptive response and completely normal. During periods of famine it will enable us to survive and maintain our vitality. If we the body doesn't know how to use its stored fat for fuel, it would perish, once it runs out of sugar.

### Indigenous Ketogenic Societies

Over the course of history, most aboriginal tribes have subsisted solely on high fat diets. In environments where there aren't many plants to be found, people rely primarily on meat.

The Innuit and Eskimos have lived off whale blubber, seal meat, salmon, cheese and caribou meat for centuries. Fat is their most precious commodity, as it gives them the extra calories they need to survive in such harsh climate. In fact, rent on land in some places is paid with butter. Despite that high amount of saturated fat and cholesterol in their diet, heart disease, diabetes and cancer were largely unknown. Only after they came in contact with white man's white refined carbohydrates did other diseases of the civilization catch up with them and they got obese.

The Masai tribe in Africa also follows a ketogenic diet. They're pastoralists and subsist mainly on their cattle, by eating their meat, drinking their unpasteurized milk and raw milk. Masai warriors are definitely a lot healthier and fitter than the majority of the people in our society.

Even in the Western world there are nations who eat a ton of fat. The Mediterranean Diet is thought to be the healthiest of them all. It consists of mainly fish, olive oil, cheese and vegetables. People from this region have less heart disease and better blood markers. Researchers from the States figured that it had to do with the low amount of saturated fat and cholesterol in their food. However, the Greek Orthodox Church also preaches a lot of fasting, which has even more profound health benefits. In fact, the more religious folk fast more than 200 days a year. This is the real cause for their vitality. As this ancient healing practice gets less popular amongst young people, disease begins to rise again because there are still a lot of refined grains and carbohydrates in the diet.

There aren't no examples of a society practicing the vegan ketogenic diet I can think of. However, I would imagine that there are vegetarians and pastoralist or fishing groups would establish a state of nutritional ketosis at least during some periods of the year, when vegetables are out of season or when it's important to keep your cattle alive.

The Vegan Keto would have to resemble a lot the Mediterranean Diet, because of its use of olives, nuts, seeds and oils.

Before the invention of agriculture and domestication of crops no hunter-gatherer community would voluntarily convert over to a solely plant based vegan diet. If they were to disregard the vast amount of calories found in animal products, then they would've starved to death or at least experienced serious malnutrition. However, in today's society we have the possibility to get all of the nutrients we need for survival from a vegan diet as well, by implementing certain useful strategies.

### *Is Ketosis Safe*

One fear that ordinary physicians have about the ketogenic diet is that it can't sustain healthy functioning of an organism. How will your body and brain survive if there are no carbohydrates?

An essential nutrient is something that's required for normal physiological functioning and the survival of the organism[iii]. It cannot be synthesized by the body and thus has to be obtained from a dietary source. Carbohydrates are non-essential, unlike amino acids and fatty acids, which we don't actually need to live and can function very well without.

Amino acids and fat are essential building blocks of all the cells in our body. Protein is used to create new muscle tissue, whereas the lipids balance our hormones that instigate these processes in the first place and protect cell membrane.

The biggest reason why we have to consume so many calories every single day is to feed our hungry brain. It comprises less than 5% of our body weight but demands about 20% of our total energy expenditure. To maintain stable blood sugar levels and a caloric balance, it needs to have access to fuel all of the time.

The brain can use only about 120 grams of glucose a day [iv], which means you still need about 30 grams of glucose while running on max ketones. That doesn't mean it ought to come from dietary carbohydrates.

During a process called *gluconeogenesis* (creation of new sugar), the liver converts amino acids found in food and glycerol, which is the backbone of triglycerides, into glucose. While in a deep fasted state, glycerol can contribute up to 21.6% of glucose production [v]. It's estimated that about 200 grams of glucose can be manufactured daily by the liver and kidneys from dietary protein and fat intake [vi].

Once you keto-adapt, your body and brain won't even need that much glucose, as they will happily use ketones instead. Carbohydrates are the default fuel source but not because they're better than fatty acids by any means. The body simply prefers it because it's easy to store and quick to absorb.

However, the brain is made up of 60% fat and runs a lot better on ketones. In fact, the high amounts of fat found in animal products and meat were probably one of the driving forces of our increased brain size. According to the Expansive Tissue Hypothesis posed by the anthropologists Leslie Aiello and Peter Wheeler suggests that the metabolic requirements of large brains were offset by a corresponding reduction of the gut[vii]. As our stomachs got smaller, our neocortices got larger. By eating solely plant foods, we wouldn't have managed to get enough excess energy for our neural network to improve itself. This doesn't necessarily mean that eating meat made us smarter. To a certain extent it did, but it wasn't the flesh but the increased amount of calories derived from fat that did. In today's world, there is an abundance of calories and therefore the vegan option is perfectly sustainable. Plant based fat sources are excellent and fit into the paradigm of ketogenic eating.

In ketosis, the brain begins to use less glucose and the small amount it needs can be derived from ketogenic foods. Muscles begin to release less glycogen as well and the entire body starts using ketones for fuel. It makes the entire organism more efficient and powerful.

## Chapter II

## *Why Do a Ketogenic Diet*

Next you might ask, why do a ketogenic diet in the first place? Veganism can be perfectly healthy if based on mainly whole foods.

Carbohydrates have gotten a bad rep in the past few years. It's not the fat either. The obesity epidemic isn't caused by one or the other macronutrient but is the culmination of many things.

But a low carb diet has been proven to be successful across many domains. There are a lot of benefits to ketosis which make it so appealing in the first place.

The most obvious advantage is increased fat oxidation[viii]. Consuming carbohydrates will make our body secrete more insulin. When this hormone is elevated we're more prone to storing rather than burning. If it's constantly high, we'll never be able to actually tap into using our own resources.

**The by-products of glucose metabolism are advanced glycation end-products (AGEs), which promote**

**inflammation and oxidative stress**[ixx], by binding a protein or lipid molecule with sugar. They speed up aging[xi], and can cause diabetes. This doesn't happen when burning clean fuel - quality fat. Also, the constantly elevated levels of circulating blood sugar are associated with nerve malfunctioning, high morbidity, bacterial infection, cancer progression and Alzheimer's.

**The #1 food for tumors is sugar.** Eating keto foods, prevents the accumulation of excess glucose in the blood, which leads to the cellular suicide of cancer. With no carbohydrates for it to feed upon, it will potentially disappear completely, at least it will diminish in size. At the same time, your healthy cells will still be nourished because they'll be using fat.

Ketosis reduces natural hunger to a bare minimum and regulates appetite[xii]. This is the result of the body being able to generate energy from both the adipose tissue and dietary fat intake. The ability to go without meals for 24 hours while not suffering any stomach pains or carb driven cravings of insanity is incredibly empowering, not to mention useful for both fitness and reducing fat composition.

Our body is made to burn fat. The adipose tissue is like a black hole with infinite storage capacity. Any surplus calorie we don't need right away gets deposited for future use. When in ketosis, we'll be withdrawing energy from our own body fat to maintain a caloric balance.

Ketones are the "superfuel" above both glucose and free fatty acids. As you can remember, they can produce 25% more energy and will cover 75% of the brains energy demands. When in ketosis you begin to need less and less glucose, which makes you more and more self-reliant.

### *Ketosis for Health*

Because of the fact that a fat molecule has twice the amount of calories than a carbohydrate it gets digested a lot slower. **Unlike sugar, that gets burned up easily, ketones move steadily and provide long lasting energy.**

This also prevents any rise in blood sugar from taking place, which happens after consuming something with a high glycemic index. Instant bursts of energy will inevitably fall as quickly. What goes up must come down. This results in hypoglycemia (a crash of blood sugar) and sleepiness. With fat that doesn't happen, as we will have an abundant fuel source, thus always feeling great. Instead of secreting insulin and taking our bodies for a rollercoaster ride, we maintain a steady stream.

**Following a low carbohydrate high fat diet has been proven very effective against a lot of the chronic illnesses people struggle with.**

- Reduction in triglycerides[xiii]

- Increase in HDL cholesterol (the good one)[xiv]

- Drop in blood pressure[xv] and insulin levels[xvi]

All of which prevent heart disease, diabetes and metabolic syndrome[xvii]. For optimal health it looks very appealing.

Mark my words when I say that ketosis will cure cancer in the near future, as it's already being used as effective treatment. At the moment science is just beginning to fully understand and utilize this metabolic state.

## *Athletes Going Against the Grain (Pun Intended)*

If you're physically active and fit, then you probably don't have to worry about obesity and other ailments. However, this doesn't mean that you can't pick up any disease or develop a severe medical condition.

Insulin resistance happens in the case of consuming too many simple carbohydrates and being constantly on a blood sugar rollercoaster ride. Even the most athletic of individuals can become diabetic and a lot of professional athletes already have.

Following a low carb diet, while still training, ought to optimize our health first and foremost. However, there are also a lot of performance enhancing benefits to using fat for fuel.

The maximum amount of glucose our bodies can store is about 2000 calories (approximately 400-500 grams of carbohydrates in the muscles, 100-150 grams in the liver and about 15 grams in the blood). Once that runs out, more fatty acids are produced to supply the demand. Although this is the point in which adipose tissue is being used it only happens to a certain degree. To still get some form of glucose, the body will also begin to break down a bit of the protein in muscles and organs to create sugar. The reason is that it's not that adapted to primarily using ketones. To prevent this from happening, a person would need to be constantly adding in more carbohydrates to fuel their activities.

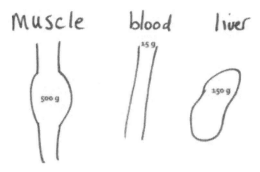

In ketosis, however, the main source of energy is significantly bigger. **Even the leanest of people with 7 % body fat carry around more than 20 000 worth of calories with them at all times.** Refeeding isn't necessary as there is always some fuel available. This also preserves muscles and other vital organs from being catabolized. Instead of being a quick sugar burner, we can become efficient fat burners instead.

Stored calories.

7%        10%

**20 000 -30 000 calories**

Ketogenic dieting is becoming very popular amongst endurance athletes, especially ultra-runners and ironman triathletes who have to perform at a high level for extreme durations. By carrying around their own fuel on their bodies they can tap into an abundance of energy. They literally go against the grain of everything in optimal sport's nutrition.

For instance, Sami Inkinen and his wife Meredith Loring rowed across the Pacific Ocean from California to Hawaii in 45 days, while following a low-carb, sugar-free, high-fat ketogenic diet. Despite being physically active for 21 hours a day, they did not suffer any decrease in performance, health or cravings for carbs. Such adaptation shows that we are capable of a lot more than we actually think. How else did our ancestors complete their epic journeys of exploration and migration across the globe?

In a study on advanced triathletes, the group who followed a ketogenic approach instead of the traditional high-carb diet showed 2-3 times higher peak fat oxidation during submaximal exercise[xviii].

Contrary to popular belief physical performance does not suffer by ditching the carbs. It is also used in strength sports such as powerlifting and gymnastics[xix] where the intensities are lot higher. Bodybuilders use periods of low-carb eating to prepare for shows and improve body composition.

In my own experience, I haven't noticed any negative side-effects of ketosis after proper adaptation. I have managed to improve every aspect of my training and health. It definitely feels great and is well worth the effort.

What about vegan ketogenic athletes? There are a lot of them who successfully follow a plant based high carb diet. However, there probably aren't any vegan keto-ers competing on the professional level. It might be impossible due to some of the shortcomings of amino acids, but clever and mindful supplementation might fix the loopholes. This entire thing is quite novel in of itself. Ketosis alone is a great performance enhancing tool but I can't tell you what the implications might be using it as a vegan. Only time can tell whether or not it can be sustainable for athletes.

### *Keto Smart*

In addition to performance oriented benefits, ketosis also has cognitive and mental ones. There's a big difference between being high on keto versus sugar.

Because of how evolutionarily valuable glucose is, the brain's reward endorphin system lights up every time we consume it, making us want more. We release a lot of the "feel-good" chemicals, such as dopamine and serotonin. Cravings and hunger pains come from some people's mind kicking into overdrive and losing their reason over something sweet.

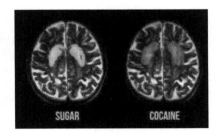

As you can see, the brain's reward system lights up the same way on sugar as it does on hard drugs. In neurological terms, binge eating and drug addiction are the same thing[xx].

This happens so that we would be motivated to repeat our actions in the future. Our taste buds are designed to recognize sweetness and fire up every single time. Feeling good after eating something sugary puts us on a short high and makes us want more.

**Sugar cravings are caused by an energy crisis in the body.** If the brain doesn't get access to fuel, it will try to motivate you to find something to eat. Because, by default, it only knows how to use glucose, it will also expect to have it.

However, if you've plugged into your largest fuel tank - your own body fat - then you won't experience these cravings. That's why people lose their sweet tooth completely when on a low carb diet. Their body detoxifies itself from sugar and the mind will get clearer.

Sugar doesn't actually provide us with that much energy and is mainly an illusion. It's a way of trapping our own ATP production. We might have a lot of stored calories but we won't be able to access them. This leads to *mental bonking* and *physical exhaustion* in everything you do, whether that be training, reading or anything else. That's why it's important to go through keto adaptation to teach the body how to use fat for fuel.

By avoiding carbohydrates, we also avoid the ups and downs of blood sugar, thus allowing our brain to function properly. By having a steady stream of energy, it doesn't have to be on the lookout for glucose. Some is indeed needed, which gets created by the liver, but the majority can be derived from ketones.

With the brain satisfied, our cognition has the opportunity to flourish. This allows us to maintain mental clarity and avoid mind fog, which accompanies the consumption of whole grains.

### *Why Fructose is Bad*

Fructose can only be metabolized by the liver and can't be used as muscle glycogen. It therefore is completely useless to the body. In high amounts it actually becomes toxic because of the liver having to work extra hard to get rid of it.

Excess fructose can damage the liver and cause insulin resistance, which means pancreas can't pump out enough insulin to lower your blood sugar. This is a precursor to diabetes, as sugar will flood your blood stream for longer and cause more damage to the blood vessels.

Fructose can also cause rapid leptin resistance. Leptin controls your appetite and metabolism. If you're resistant, then you'll gain weight easily and can't stop gorging yourself.

The reaction of fructose with proteins is 7 times higher than with glucose. AGEs get produced at an even greater rate. While your body can't use fructose as energy, the bad bacteria in your gut can and that can cause imbalances in your healthy gut flora.

What's more, it also causes oxidative stress and inflammation. Cancer cells feed upon sugar, especially fructose and thrive in an oxidized environment.

Excess fructose also affects brain functioning, in terms of appetite regulation and blood sugar. In rats, it impairs memory.

On a fat burning metabolism, we can think more clearly and with less disruption. Our ability to concentrate increases and I dare say that so does our intelligence. Who knows, maybe our IQ does so as well. Not directly, but as a result of being able to allocate our psychic energy into appropriate channels and activities that make us smarter. Personally, I've definitely noticed a lot of improvement in this area.

### *Sleep Like the Sleeping Beauty*

Additionally, the quality of our sleep improves because of the stability in blood sugar. If we run out of glucose in the middle of the night, then we will become hypoglycemic. Our starving brain will wake us up to get some fuel for survival. Midnight snacking is another example of people feeding all of the time and a bad habit to have.

Constant stream of energy means that there's no need to recharge as much, resulting in quality slumber. This way we can go through full sleep cycles and actually enter the deepest stages of recovery where all dreaming occurs and the magic happens. During my own periods of ketosis, I've gone through the entire night like a log without waking up.

Sleep is one of the most important things for building muscle, getting stronger and burning fat. During the day we're exposing our body to all types of exhausting activities that push our limits to the extreme. Stress, exercise, thinking, traffic, mental algorithms, situational awareness, cognitive sharpness etc. are all draining us and not something we're supposed to be facing with on a daily basis. To actually cause enhanced physiological adaptations we have to allow the recovery processes to happen.

**What you will also see is that you get less tired overall when on keto.** Physical activities become less demanding and your endurance will increase by default. If you're obese, then you'll reclaim your enthusiasm and vitality for life. Being overweight means that you should be immediately put on a low carb diet. Physiologically, it doesn't make sense to keep playing with insulin and sugar.

But isn't fat bad for our health? Definitely not. This fat-phobia is the result of false and biased science which based their results on studies with the wrong context.

## *The Big Fat Lies and Myths Debunked*

Veganism and not eating animal products doesn't equal health or weight loss. If you eat crap your body will still get diseased and obese. That's why you shouldn't expect any diet program to be a magic pill and still have to put in the effort. Vegans are reported to be healthier, but that's not because of what they eat, but because they're already a lot more mindful of their eating habits in the first place.

Of course, fat is dangerous with elevated levels of insulin. During glycation sugar and fat molecules attach to each other, that create AGEs, and begin to circulate the blood stream for a longer period of time. This will cause oxidation and impairs the functioning of biomolecules. Doing this kills our mitochondria and causes cellular death. It also speeds up aging and will most definitely lead to disease.

Nutritional ketosis alters our metabolism completely and makes us use various fuel sources completely differently. **Keto adaptation increases the rate at which the body burns saturated fat for fuel and maintains better overall glucose levels.**

Fat in of itself is actually a lot better for us as it's vital for a lot of hormonal production and is more satiating. Saturated fat is needed for our neurotransmitters to work, making it essential for cognitive health and performance. We just must not mix it together with carbohydrates, ever.

The type of fat eaten is also important. In ketosis you're under different metabolic conditions than with a high carbohydrate diet. When fat is used for fuel, the body prefers more quality mono-unsaturates and saturates. As a sugar burner those things may not be as appealable.

The fatty parts of the animal are more nutritious and were valued most by hunter-gatherers. Indigenous people with unprocessed high meat diets were perfectly healthy, until they came in contact with the food industries of the West. The combination of their traditional way of eating and the introduction of refined carbohydrates resulted in disease, tooth decay and obesity[xxi]. Of course, on the vegan approach you won't be eating meat, but it doesn't mean that you can't consume saturated fat or cholesterol.

**Another depicted villain is cholesterol** which is produced by the body and needed for cell walls, bile production, vitamin D, brain and nerve functioning and hormonal production. It's an essential structural component of all animal cell membranes. Consumption of cholesterol does not increase it because of the feedback mechanism. There is no good or bad cholesterol, simply in a specific context it rises too high and becomes lethal.

Plant based foods don't have high amounts of cholesterol. Studies have shown that vegan diets tend to have lower levels of it in general. It's not a bad thing nor is it particularly good either. On a low carb high fat eating plan you may actually increase your HDL (the good one) by consuming more saturated fats.

**One more fear is salt.** Sodium intake necessary for human life especially on the ketogenic diet. Again, it's the wrong context that creates all of the problems and dangers. High carbohydrate intake makes the kidneys retain salt, whereas a low carb diet increases sodium exertion by the kidney (called the natriuresis of fasting).

Once you go through the shift and eat appropriately, your body will heal itself. Inflammation disappears and you'll have less aches and pains. You may think that it's normal to be feeling the way you do now, but that's because you don't know that there's another way.

All of these benefits are the reason why you should try a ketogenic diet... at least once. It will give you high end physical as well as cognitive performance and is incredibly healthy.

Being in this metabolic state is very advantageous, as we become more resourceful with our own supplies and can thus always be excelling at whatever we're doing. You're going to have to keep it a secret, but the military is also very interested of ketosis and is actively testing it on topnotch soldiers. When on keto, we literally can become Superhuman even as a vegan.

# Chapter III

## How to Get into Ketosis

## Vegan Style

Nutritional ketosis goes against the grain (pun intended) and contradicts almost everything that is considered to be healthy nowadays. While the standard guidelines recommend about 50-60% of carbohydrates, ketogenic diets remain under 5%. Instead, what gets used the most is fat, making up to 70-80% of the macronutrient ratios.

What's more, typical vegans use the 80/10/10 approach and eat 80% carbs. On a whole foods diet with plant based foods it might be healthy, but if you were to consume refined grains, sugars, pastry etc., then you would severely damage your health.

You as a ketogenic vegan will definitely be an anomaly and the pioneer of an upcoming movement. It seems impossible to fit within the macros of keto, but it's possible.

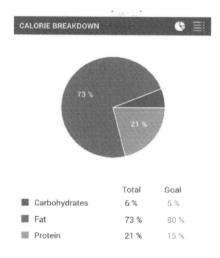

| | Total | Goal |
|---|---|---|
| ■ Carbohydrates | 6 % | 5 % |
| ■ Fat | 73 % | 80 % |
| ▨ Protein | 21 % | 15 % |

### *The Foods Eaten on a Plant Based High Fat Diet*

The food on a ketogenic diet is mostly animal based. Most of the calories come from either meat, fish, eggs or other rich sources of fat such as butter. As a vegan all of those things are non-negotiable. Because this book is about vegan keto, we'll be eating only plant based foods.

**To induce ketosis insulin needs to be suppressed for an extended period of time.** As a result, glucagon goes up and starts to empty the liver's glycogen stores. This is achieved by using our current storage and not eating high glycemic carbohydrates that raise our blood sugar even before we can put them into our mouth. Protein does so as well but to a much lesser degree and more steadily. Add fat into the mix and it will happen even more slowly. Leafy green vegetables are also safe as the actual amount of sugar in them is small in comparison to their fiber content, which decreases the rate of absorption. That's what you should be primarily consuming.

### *Carbohydrates*

Total caloric proportion is less than 5 %. In total, the carbohydrate intake would be around 30 grams, fiber not included. The less of them, the faster will ketosis be induced. On the other hand, vegan keto-ers may find this unachievable. All plant based foods have carbs in them. So, increasing your daily intake only slightly up to about 50 grams may be useful. However, during the adaptation phase you want to stay as low as possible. Otherwise you won't be able to get into ketosis the first time.

Safe sources are fibrous leafy green and cruciferous vegetables, such as

| Food | Amount | Fat | NET Carbs (g) | Protein (g) |
|---|---|---|---|---|
| Lettuce, Butterhead | 2oz/56 grams | 0 | 0.5 | 1 |
| Beet Greens | 2oz/56 grams | 0 | 0.5 | 1 |
| Bok Choy | 2oz/56 grams | 0 | 0.5 | 1 |
| Spinach | 2oz/56 grams | 0 | 1 | 1.5 |
| Alfalfa Sprouts | 2oz/56 grams | 0 | 1 | 2 |

| | | | | |
|---|---|---|---|---|
| Swiss Chard | 2oz/56 grams | 0 | 1 | 1 |
| Arugula | 2oz/56 grams | 0 | 1 | 1.5 |
| Celery | 2oz/56 grams | 0 | 1 | 0.5 |
| Lettuce | 2oz/56 grams | 0 | 1 | 0.5 |
| Asparagus | 2oz/56 grams | 0 | 1 | 1 |
| Eggplant | 2oz/56 grams | 0 | 1 | 0.5 |

| | | | | |
|---|---|---|---|---|
| Mushrooms, White | 2oz/56 grams | 0 | 1.5 | 2 |
| Tomatoes | 2oz/56 grams | 0 | 1 | 0.5 |
| Cauliflower | 2oz/56 grams | 0 | 1.5 | 1 |
| Green Bell Pepper | 2oz/56 grams | 0 | 1.5 | 0.5 |
| Cabbage | 2oz/56 grams | 0 | 2 | 1 |
| Broccoli | 2oz/56 grams | 0 | 2 | 1.5 |

| | | | | |
|---|---|---|---|---|
| Green Beans | 2oz/56 grams | 0 | 2 | 1 |
| Brussels Sprouts | 2oz/56 grams | 0 | 2.5 | 1.5 |
| Kale | 2oz/56 grams | 0 | 2 | 2 |
| Artichoke | 2oz/56 grams | 0 | 2.5 | 2 |
| Kelp | 2oz/56 grams | 0 | 3 | 1 |
| Zucchini | 2oz/56 grams | 0 | 2 | 1 |

There are also a small variety of fruits and berries you can consume.

| Food | Amount | Fat (g) | NET Carbs (g) | Protein (g) |
|---|---|---|---|---|
| Rhubarb | 100 grams | 0 | 2 | 1 |
| Raspberries | 100 grams | 0 | 5 | 1.5 |
| Blueberries | 100 grams | 0 | 10 | 2 |
| Strawberries | 100 grams | 0 | 5 | 1 |
| Blackberries | 100 grams | 0 | 5 | 1.5 |

**Top 5 recommendations are:**

- Spinach
- Kelp
- Broccoli
- Cauliflower
- Cabbage

## _Protein_

Total caloric proportion at about 15 %. Herein lies the biggest issue of a vegan keto diet. It's thought to be impossible to get enough protein by eating only plant based foods.

We don't actually need as much protein as we think – it's the protein myth. In fact, when in ketosis our overall demands for it get reduced even lower. We don't need more than 0.7-1 grams per pound of lean body weight. Even less, if you're sedentary. An active person should get a bit more.  Still, it's important to get in all of the essential amino acids, which is quite difficult to do as a vegan. That's why you should consume a variety of nutrients.

All plant based foods have protein in them. Also, there are plenty of meat substitutes out there. However, packaged products tend to also have a higher carb content, so read your labels carefully.

| Food | Amount | Fat (g) | NET carbs (g) | Protein (g) |
|------|--------|---------|---------------|-------------|
|      |        |         |               |             |

| | | | | |
|---|---|---|---|---|
| Tofu, Calcium Sulfate, Firm | 100 grams | 9 | 2 | 16 |
| Tofu, Nigari, Hard | 100 grams | 10 | 3 | 13 |
| Pumpkin Seeds | 28 grams/1oz | 6 | 3 | 10 |
| Tofu, Silken Extra Firm | 100 grams | 2 | 2 | 7 |
| Almonds | 28 grams/1oz | 15 | 2 | 6 |
| Almond Flour | 28 grams/1oz | 14 | 3 | 6 |
| Tofu, Silken, Soft | 100g | 3 | 3 | 5 |

| | | | | |
|---|---|---|---|---|
| Flax Seeds | 28 grams/1oz | 12 | 1 | 5 |
| Chia Seeds | 28 grams/1oz | 9 | 1 | 4 |
| Brazil Nuts | 28 grams/1oz | 19 | 2 | 4 |
| Hazelnuts | 28 grams/1oz | 17 | 2 | 4 |
| Walnuts | 28 grams/1oz | 18 | 2 | 4 |
| Pecans | 28 grams/1oz | 20 | 1 | 3 |
| Coconut, unsweetened | 28 grams/1oz | 18 | 2 | 2 |

| | | | | |
|---|---|---|---|---|
| Macadamia Nuts | 28 grams/1oz | 21 | 2 | 2 |
| Green Peas | 100 grams | 0 | 6 | 5 |
| Soybeans | 100 grams | 20 | 20 | 36 |

There are also great plant based protein supplements with a low carb content. If you need some more protein to meet your daily requirements, then you can use some great organic green powders, plant based rice protein or hemp protein. Just fit it into your macros.

**Top 5 recommendations are:**

- Silken Tofu
- Organic Nigari Tofu
- Almonds
- Chia Seeds
- Pumpkin Seeds

## Fats

To be honest, there isn't actually a limit to how much fat we should be consuming. The more of it, the more ketones will be produced. With no carbohydrates in the menu, we need to have another fuel source for the body.

In order to get into ketosis, we need to eat fat and a lot of it. What I'm talking about is adding it on our vegetables, protein, coffee - everywhere. Most commonly, it's found in butter, lard and heavy cream. But luckily, there are a lot of plant based sources as well.

| Food | Amount | Fat (g) | NET Carbs (g) | Protein |
|------|--------|---------|---------------|---------|
| Avocado Oil | 28 grams/1oz | 28 | 0 | 0 |
| Cocoa Butter | 28 grams/1oz | 28 | 0 | 0 |

| | | | | |
|---|---|---|---|---|
| Coconut Oil | 28 grams/1oz | 28 | 0 | 0 |
| Flaxseed Oil | 28 grams/1oz | 28 | 0 | 0 |
| Macadamia Oil | 28 grams/1oz | 28 | 0 | 0 |
| MCT Oil | 28 grams/1oz | 28 | 0 | 0 |
| Olive Oil | 28 grams/1oz | 28 | 0 | 0 |
| Red Palm Oil | 28 grams/1oz | 28 | 0 | 0 |
| Coconut Cream | 28 grams/1oz | 10 | 1 | 1 |

| | | | | |
|---|---|---|---|---|
| Olives | 28 grams/1oz | 4 | 0.5 | 1 |
| Avocados | 28 grams/1oz | 4 | 2 | 1 |
| Coconut Milk | 28 grams/1oz | 7 | 1 | 1 |
| Almond Butter | 28 grams/1oz | 18 | 2 | 7 |
| Brazil Nuts | 28 grams/1oz | 19 | 1 | 4 |

Top 5 recommendations are:

- Organic Extra Virgin Coconut Oil
- Extra Virgin Olive Oil
- Macadamia Nut Oil
- Premium Avocado Oil
- Unroasted Brazil Nuts

What ought to be avoided are refined vegetable oils and trans fats, such as rapeseed oil, canola oil, margarine etc. They are more inflammatory and actually dangerous for our health. Also, the biggest reason why saturated fat is considered bad in the first place.

Getting into nutritional ketosis isn't easy. Initially, the body will reject this new fuel source and keeps on wanting to satisfy its glucose addiction. Sugar feeds parasites and promotes yeast infection in our gut. Having a big sweet tooth is the result of just that. The more we eat it the more we actually begin to crave because of certain dopamine receptors in our brain.

Simple carbohydrates make us want more of this stimulus by causing a rewarding feeling. Abstaining from sugar cleanses the body and liberates the mind from craving it. While in nutritional ketosis we're completely free from anything like that. The food we eat is already incredibly satisfying and we don't need anything sweetened.

## *Symptoms of Withdrawal*

The biggest reason why the majority either fail or don't even start a ketogenic diet is that they are afraid of it.

After years of being fed a whole-grain diet and villainizing fat, they think that they're going to have a heart attack. Of course, if you were to eat randomly and not ditch the carbs, then you're going to have a bad time.

If they have decided to try it out, then they will also come across a lot of negative side effects. **The process of adaptation takes at least 2-3 weeks.** At first, you won't be able to experience almost any of the benefits, but will suffer from withdrawal symptoms.

This "keto flu" happens because the body doesn't know how to use fat for fuel. The brain will be screaming for energy and demands glucose. Eating carbs will put a cold halt to inducing ketosis and prevents any metabolic change.

This is where patience and perseverance come into play. The severity of it will depend on how addicted to sugar your body has been before. If you come from the background of the SAD diet, then it will take you longer than someone who is used to eating Paleo and already used to less sugar.

Chances are that you're currently a high carb vegan. This might cause you some additional headaches but nothing too severe. Jumping over to almost zero carbohydrates will definitely be a shock to the body, but it's going to be that of a good kind. Your adaptation may be slightly longer but follow all of the tips I'm going to share with you and it will be a breeze.

During that period there will be some uncomfortable signs of withdrawal, such as dizziness, fatigue, slight headaches and the feeling of being hit with a club, which all pass away after a while.

### *Am I in Ketosis?*

To know whether or not you're in ketosis you can measure your blood ketones using <u>Ketostix</u>. Optimal measurements are between 0,5 and 3,0 mMol. The same can be done with a <u>glucometer</u>. If you're fasting blood glucose is under 80 mg/dl and you're not feeling hypoglycemic then you're probably in ketosis. Ketoacidocis occurs over 10mMol, which is quite hard to reach.

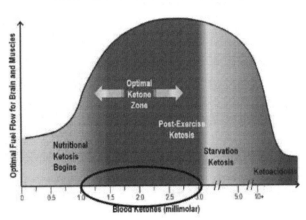

## What level of Ketosis is optimal?

Page 91: The Art and Science of Low Carbohydrate Performance
Jeff S. Volek and Stephen D. Phinney

| BLOOD GLUCOSE CHART | | | |
|---|---|---|---|
| Mg/DL | Fasting | After Eating | 2-3 hours After Eating |
| Normal | 80-100 | 170-200 | 120-140 |
| Impaired Glucose | 101-125 | 190-230 | 140-160 |
| Diabetic | 126+ | 220-300 | 200 plus |

**But there are a few problems with measuring ketones.**

- Having elevated levels of ketones doesn't mean you're in ketosis.
- These urine strips are expensive and taking several measurements a day is very costly.

That's why we there's another way how to know you're in ketosis without strips. Elevated ketone levels don't necessarily mean ketosis. It might even be the opposite.

If we're not putting that fuel into use, then we're probably urinating it out. That's why urine strips are not ideal.

What we want to know as well is our blood sugar levels. Glucose and ketones are contradicting fuel sources. If one is elevated, then the other has to be decreased.

If we have high blood sugar levels, then we won't be able to use fat for fuel. We definitely won't be in ketosis.

**There are a lot of additional symptoms of ketosis that occur during adaptation.**

### *Water weight loss*

The biggest of which is probably fluid retention, or in this case, lack thereof. Carbohydrate molecules are very prone to binding together with liquids. Our body is made up of a lot of water and therefore can store a lot of it in our muscles.

Once you start restricting your carb intake, you'll lose a lot of water weight. It's not fat necessarily but just your excess sugar being flushed out.

### *You're thirsty*

What will follow is also increased thirst. This is caused by a loss in water weight to a certain extent. In addition to that, you'll want to drink more water because your body needs it.

The more water you drink, the less of it your body will store. While eating carbs, you're prone to depositing fluids because of increased liquid retention. Once you get flushed, you will be slightly dehydrated and have to compensate for it with increased water intake. You were dehydrated previously as well. It's just that carbs prevented you from getting that thirsty.

Drink a lot of water. At least 8 cups a day. On a ketogenic diet or eating low carb, even more.

### Keto breath

The most infamous symptom of ketosis is a smelly mouth. Once you're stored carbohydrates have been depleted you begin to use more fat for fuel.

During lipolysis (burning fatty acids in the Krebs cycle) we create a ketone body called acetone. Instead of using it for energy, we'll be excreting most of it in our urine and breath. That's how Ketostix work as well.

The smell is often described as "fruity", acidic or slightly rotten. If you've got an upcoming date, then be wary.

### Metallic taste in your mouth

Because of the same reason we'll be having a slightly metallic or sweet taste in our mouth. It's acetone leaving its mark in our saliva and breath.

### Stinky urine

Acetone again being excreted by the body. The odor is quite strong. To be honest, it smells like acidic death. Your sweat can also have the same effects.

Because you'll be flushing out water, you'll experience urinating more often as well. Stay hydrated.

### Slight headaches and fatigue

During keto adaptation your body is going through a slight energy crisis. It still wants to use glucose but there's none around. It doesn't know how to burn fat for fuel yet and is therefore making you feel exhausted.

The initial period may cause headaches, sugar cravings, lethargy and muscle fatigue. Don't worry, these side effects will all pass away once you get fat adapted. This is also what makes people shy away from ketosis the most. They just don't have the patience.

### Lack of appetite

Next to all of these slightly uncomfortable symptoms, there are also amazing ones. The best of which is reduced appetite. You'll be eating a lot of fat, protein and fibrous vegetables, which are the most satiating nutrients.

Because of that you'll almost never feel hungry and are constantly satisfied with your meals. You won't have to eat as often as well, because of your body burning fat for fuel.

### After Adaptation

If you've eaten low carb for about 2-3 weeks, then you're probably in ketosis. At some point, you'll start to feel a lot better. In fact, better than ever before.

You'll experience.

- No hunger whatsoever.
- Mental clarity.
- High levels of energy at all times.
- Increased endurance.
- Reduced inflammation

- Reduced bloating.

- No sugar cravings.

- Improved sleep.

- Stable blood sugar levels.

- No muscle catabolism.

- Less fatigue during exercise, any other time as well, really.

This is what to expect once you've become fat adapted. You can use Ketostix to measure your progress. But it doesn't necessarily mean you're in ketosis *per se*. Follow your intuition first and foremost.

### *Do I Have to be in Ketosis?*

Quantifying and measuring can turn into an obsession. Trust me, it's very frustrating to not see your blood glucose levels not being where you want them to be despite trying very hard. It can cause a lot of stress. At least that's how I felt during my initial adaptation period. That's why I wanted to show you how to get into ketosis without losing your mind.

To be honest, it doesn't matter whether or not you're in ketosis. It's not a magic pill that immediately turns you into a superhuman. Nor is it a badge of honor that you could wear. *"Oh, look at me, my blood ketone levels are in the optimal zone. Therefore, I'm better than you!"*

In my opinion we don't need nor should want to be in ketosis all of the time. It's a great tool to have in our metabolic arsenal but not the only one. I love eating keto because of how it makes me feel.

**Unless you're diabetic or have any other medical condition, then you shouldn't worry about getting kicked out of ketosis.**

Nutritional ketosis *per se* isn't the purpose of health and well-being. Being fat adapted and burning fat for fuel is a lot more important. This can be achieved by eating low carb as well. However, the initial period of keto adaptation is necessary for these pathways to be created.

## Chapter IV

## Mistakes to Avoid

Nutritional ketosis isn't easy. The adaptation process takes time and at first you have to be very meticulous. Even seemingly innocent mistakes can do a lot of damage and will prevent you from making progress. Afterwards you don't have to be as strict and it will be all worth it. The more your body knows how to use fat for fuel the better it gets.

In my own experience, there are an array of things that could go wrong. Thanks to many self-experiments, I've managed to find every potential problem and also solve them. On the vegan keto diet there are even more things to remember. Obviously, you can't be eating meat, but there are several other important factors that have to be kept in mind.

### Too Many Carbs to Adapt

The biggest mistake we could make is to consume too many carbohydrates. They need to be restricted to less than 30 grams per day, without the fiber, for our body to enter ketosis.

The problem with most low carb diets is that they do not restrict their sugar intake enough for the body to completely convert over to fat burning. Consuming even slightly too much will keep us on the peripheral areas of keto adaptation. This is the worst place to be in because we will not be able to shift our metabolism into efficiently using ketones or get enough energy from glucose.

To get the most out of that amount we ought to be consuming only green leafy vegetables and not waste our allowance on things that don't satiate us as much.

Sugar hides itself in all shapes and form. Processed meat substitutes usually have added wheat or are cured in dextrose. Even though some foods might be keto friendly, such as nuts and tofu, they still have a significant amount of sugar in them. Protein powders are the same. That is why it's important to read the labels of everything that has one, as they can potentially spike our insulin. It almost resembles deciphering the complex linguistics of some ancient tablets.

# *How to Read Nutrition Labels*

There are some national variations in terms of terminology, quantities and legislations but the core principles remain the same as long as we interpret the data according to our individual context. Put on your Indiana Jones' hat because this requires a lot of deciphering and linguistic work.

This is just a random example about what's most relevant and will guide you to making better decisions.

1. **The serving information.** We'll start from the very top. This will tell you the size of a single serving and the total amount of them per package. These are random

measurements not recommendations and the food companies can use them to trick uneducated readers.

2. **Calories per serving.** A bag of chips may have only 100 calories per serving, but the entire bag has 5 of them, totaling in 500 calories. I wouldn't bother making real interpretations based solely on this. The best way to understand this data is to adjust it to 100 grams instead.

3. **Macronutrient ratios.** Next check out all of the macros. It's important to also see what proportions each of them contain. Be aware of the amount of trans fats and sugars. In the case of carbohydrates note how much of it is fiber as it may differ from the actual soluble content. I would completely ignore the % of daily values because the public recommendations are not individualized and taken out of context. It's based on an average 2000 calorie diet and might be completely the opposite to what we need. We only want to know the amounts we will be consuming and adjust that according to our own demands.

**4. Micronutrients.** The same applies to the vitamins. There is not much use to knowing how many micronutrients we're getting. If anything, then they're more likely put there to distract the reader away from all of the other potential hazards and bring in more confusion. Our individual deficiencies play a role here as well and we don't necessarily need everything.

**5. Ingredients.** They have to be listed in order of quantity with the major ones coming first. Some of them should also have exact percentages and amounts. All of the allergens or hazards are bolded for faster recognition but it varies between countries. Make sure you read and understand all of them and steer away from the dangers.

In the United States if a food has less than 0,5 grams of trans fat in a serving, the label can have 0 grams of it. This hidden sources will add up if you eat too much and can be the hidden source of your problems. That's why it's important to also check the ingredient list for the actual contents for hydrogenated fats and vegetable oils.

Additionally, what needs to be counted towards the daily carbohydrate allowance is seasoning. Industrialized mixes like lemon pepper or table salt are already contaminated with dextrose and, therefore, ought to be avoided like wildfire.

Natural spices, like cinnamon, turmeric and ginger also have a minute carbohydrate content. We should be using them for their other medicinal benefits but be careful not to go overboard. This was one of the missing pieces of the puzzle that slowed down my adaptation the first time. I used to sprinkle seasoning on everything but didn't count them towards my daily carb allowance.

**List of foods to avoid:**

- All types of tubers, such as carrots, turnips, beetroot, potatoes.
- All grain products, such as rice, flour, wheat, barley, rye, quinoa.
- All legumes and lentils.
- All fruit, such as bananas, apples, oranges, grapes, watermelon etc.

- No yogurt with added sugar, no sodas, no milk, no chocolate, no cookies, no chips etc.

### *Too Much Protein – Highly Unlikely*

After eating too many carbohydrates, the next possible thing that hinders adaptation would be *glyconeogenesis*. Eating too much protein can convert even the juiciest of stakes into cake in our blood stream. What you don't need right away gets turned into sugar because during withdrawal every ounce of glucose is valuable. The body will sniff out whatever it can find.

However, for that to happen we would have to be consuming quite a lot. On a vegan diet you don't have to worry about this as much. Plants don't have that much protein in them. Nevertheless, you can still potentially eat too much tofu or protein powder.

You want to get as much protein with as little amount of carbohydrates as possible. Leafy green vegetables have some protein in them, but to meet your daily requirements, without exceeding your carb allowance is difficult. You don't want to waste anything.

The recommended daily allowance for protein is already very low in comparison to what we would benefit from. How much we need depends on our weight and activity levels.

A sedentary person doesn't need nearly as much as someone who trains hard. If you're a small woman, then your requirements would be less than 100 grams per day. However, an athlete ought to be minimally consuming 0.8 grams per pound of lean body mass or 2 grams per kilogram, which is quite low and not nearly as much as the bodybuilding gurus tell us to eat.

**The maximum we could get away with would be 1 g/pound.** Anything higher than that will potentially turn into sugar.

Ketosis is actually protein sparing because of the constant anabolic state we're in. Muscles will always have enough calories around and don't need to break down the body's own tissue and organs for energy.

After you've become fat adapted you don't have to worry about this as much. If you eat too much protein you'll get kicked out of ketosis, but only for a short period of time. Once a few hours have passed you'll re-enter the fat burning zone.

## Not Enough Fat...What?

Another mistake would be not eating enough fat. As weird as it might sound that could happen. By eliminating carbohydrates from the menu we need to have another fuel source to feed our hungry brain. This means putting oil over everything. The lethargy and fatigue can be minimized by not adding caloric restriction on top of the adaptation process.

If we give our body more fat, it will inevitably have to accept it. Moreover, this will also promote the liver's production of additional ketone bodies. To be honest, there isn't a limit to how much fat we should consume. The more we do, the better for the induction of ketosis. What needs to be avoided, however, are the wrong types of fats, such as vegetable oils and trans fats, because of their inflammatory properties.

After all of the other macronutrients have been dialed in and potential infiltrations of sugar removed it's only a matter of time. It takes a lot of patience to get into ketosis. Quantifying with Ketostix or a glucometer would tell us about our progress but we shouldn't get caught up with the numbers. We can easily become consumed by it which would make things only worse.

## *Additional Factors*

During the initial adaptation phase, we want to keep our stress levels as low as possible because it will stop us from adjusting to this massive change our body is going through. Quality nutrition, sleep, hydration, fresh air, exercise, being calm and centered are especially important at that time.

**Drinking more than adequate amounts of water is very important.** Carbs make the body hold onto liquids more easily because of their molecular structure. Once we deprive ourselves from glucose we will flush out a lot of water weight. This is perfectly normal but to prevent any negative consequences of that, we need to increase our hydration.

The recommendation is about 8 cups of water a day but it's not enough on keto. Drink at least 10 cups a day. At the same time, listen to your intuition and also look at the color of your urine. If you're not thirsty, then don't feel obligated to drink more water.

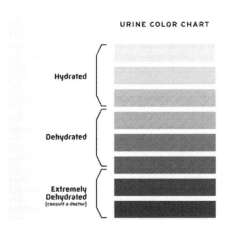

**Additionally, mineral intake with sodium is also vital.** Electrolyte deficiencies will lead to muscle cramping, headaches and too much stress.

What's more, drinking too much water and peeing may make us excrete out our electrolytes more than we consume. That's why you should pay close attention to your urine color and how often you tend to go to the bathroom. If you do it every hour, then dial back on your water intake.

To make sure we keep things in check, we can drink water with a bit of good quality salt in it to improve our hydration and reduce cortisol levels, especially if we do it first thing in the morning.

**One of the biggest things that gets neglected in our modern wired up lives is sleep.** It's the time during which our body conducts all of its repair processes. Growth hormone is also released the most during the first few hours of shut-eye at about 11 PM.

Make sure you get about 7-8 hours of sleep a night because anything less will cause too much stress to the body. Inadequate amounts will lead to insulin resistance, too high blood glucose levels, fatigue, fat accumulation and muscle waste.

The best advice I can give you is to adjust your sleeping schedule to the circadian rhythm. This might not be possible but it's the ideal worth striving towards. The most optimal time to go to bed is at about 10PM. Waking up depends, but cortisol starts raising at about 5-7AM to wake us up naturally.

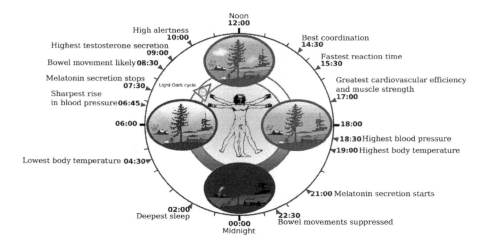

To make sure you get a good night's sleep, you have to block out blue light exposure from your gadgets and technology. It will keep our subconscious mind up and suppresses melatonin, which is the sleep hormone. Start wearing blue light blocking glasses after 8PM and install a software called Flux on your computer.

First thing in the morning after waking up, you should drink at least 1 cup of water with about ½ teaspoons of either sea salt or rock salt in it. Make sure you mix it nicely with a spoon before because it will make the sodium crystals blend in with the liquid.

Therefore, we should maintain this zen-like attitude towards the whole experience and simply let things everything run their course. Rather than being frustrated or lethargic we have to accept it as it is. We can't control what happens to us but only our response to it.

Don't turn into an angry vegan who's aggressively and neurotically obsessing over their nutritional philosophy. Do support your cause but don't get too crazy either.

It ought to be something we enjoy and can later reflect back upon as an opportunity to learn more about our own body. Don't stress out on your ketone levels either. There isn't a specific point where we will become fat adapted but eventually we'll simply get accustomed to this new alteration of our own biology.

# Chapter V

## Intermittent Fasting

A healthy lifestyle should also include some abstention from food. Fasting induces ketosis very rapidly within 2-3 days and is the most natural and quickest ways of doing it.

Ketone bodies may rise up to 70-fold during prolonged fasting[xxii]. Fasting also skyrockets human growth hormone exponentially within the first few days to maintain lean body mass and muscle tissue. Afterwards it does so less significantly because protein catabolism gets reduced to almost non-existent levels. In this state, the majority of the body's energy demands will be met by the use of free fatty acids and ketones.

Physiologically, fasting and ketosis are the 2 sides of the same coin. However, there are even more benefits that are characteristic specifically to fasting.

**The benefits of intermittent fasting:**

- Cellular repair and detoxification through a pathway called autophagy, which removes waste material from cells[xxiii]
- Increased metabolism by 3.6-14% after 48 hours[xxiv]
- More insulin sensitivity[xxv]
- Human growth hormone gets skyrocketed by 1300-2000%[xxvi]
- Increased longevity and lifespan
- Cancer and tumor protection
- Bolstered brain power and protection against neurodegenerative disease

As you can see, most of the benefits, *sans autophagy,* can be achieved on a well-formulated ketogenic diet as well.

There are several ways we can structure our intermittent fasting.

Actually, it doesn't even matter when, as long as you simply do it. The length of the fast isn't as important either. After a certain amount of time we'll have reaped all of the benefits and can stop fasting, without going through several days.

**Here are a few ways of doing it.**

- **24-hour fast.** This is the most basic way. It doesn't even have to mean that you actually go through a day without eating. Simply have dinner in the evening, fast throughout the next day and eat dinner again. This one is also prescribed by the author of _Eat Stop Eat_ Brad Pilon. The frequency depends on the person but once or twice a week should be the golden standard. An active person who trains hard should do it less often than a sedentary person.

- **16/8 time frame every day.** This is my favorite strategy, popularized by Martin Berkhan, which I'm doing daily. You fast for 16 hours and have a feeding window of 8. Simply skip breakfast and have it during lunch instead. By that time all of the HGH and other hormonal benefits will have reached their peak. It's also the time where our body has managed to digest and remove all of the food and waste from the previous day. In my opinion, we should all be following this. It's an optimal way of eating by consuming food only when it's necessary. We don't even have to be as strict with it. Instead of following 16/8 we can do 14/10, 18/6, 20/4 or whatever fits the situation. The point is to simply reduce the amount of time we spend in a fed state and to be fasting for the majority of the day.

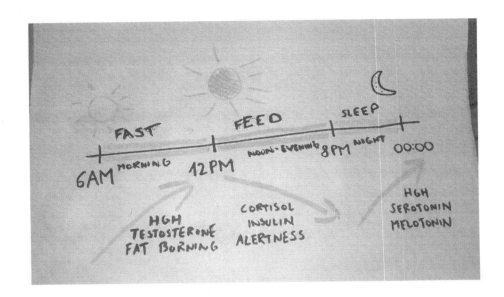

- **The Warrior Diet** is a fasting protocol created by Ori Hofmekler. The entire concept is based around ancient warrior nations, such as the Spartans and Romans, who would be physically active throughout the day and only eat at night. At daylight they would only get a few bites here and there and would consume a lot of calories in the evening. This diet follows the 20/4 timeframe with one massive meal eaten at dinner.

- **Fasting for several days**. Although very effective for weight loss, I don't see immense benefits in doing this for healthy individuals. Autophagy and detoxification will certainly increase but I would like to think that similar results will be achieved with daily intermittent fasting, such as the 16/8 window. The frequency might actually be a lot better than the intensity. However, doing a fast for several days at least once a year sounds like a wise idea, as it will completely detoxify the body and will also clear metal toxicity.

- **Breakfast and dinner.** As a final resort you can follow the pattern of 50-50, meaning you have breakfast early in the morning, go through the day without eating and have dinner. This way you'll fast for about 8-10 hours and actually do it twice in one 24-hour period. It's not ideal but still better than 6 meals a day. At least you'll be able to not become too dependent of the food and can get the most of the benefits.

There are also approaches like _The 5:2 Diet_ and _Alternate Day Fasting_, which include fasting but allow the consumption of about 500 calories on days of abstention. I wouldn't recommend this, because caloric restriction won't allow all of the physiological benefits of fasting to kick in. You want to shock the body and go straight to zero for the greatest effects.

Based on my research and experimentation, the most effective way to do this is through _Intermittent Fasting and Feasting_, which is also the title of one the books I've written about the topic. In its core, it resembles a lot the Warrior Diet, but is slightly different. It's actually better, because it incorporates periods of undereating and overfeeding with nutritional ketosis.

Basically, you skip breakfast, fast for about 15-17 hours until noon and have a very small ketogenic meal of about 300-500 calories. As a result, the insignificant impact on blood sugar levels will prolong your fasting period even further and makes you more ketogenic. After that, you wait about 5-6 hours and have a big dinner. You'll still be eating keto foods but in larger quantities.

**The advantage to this is 3-fold.**

- By skipping breakfast, you allow your body to conduct detoxifying and autophagy.

- At noon, your HGH production will have increased and having a small meal will give you more energy to.

- Keeping yourself slightly underfed throughout the day sends a signal to the body to speed up nutrient partitioning and protein synthesis. By overfeeding at dinner you'll utilize your food more efficiently and supercompensate for the abstinence.

**Another thing to consider is protein fasting.** In a nutshell, you occasionally reduce your daily protein intake dramatically, almost to a zero. It's a great tool to reduce inflammation, kick-start weight loss and to protect yourself against tumors, cancer and aging.

By doing protein fasting once a week, you're allowing your body to induce *autophagy*. You'll be self-digesting your own tissue. It might seem like you're cannibalizing yourself and starving, but in reality *autophagy* is required to maintain lean body mass and it actually inhibits the breakdown of muscle in adults[xxvii].

It also improves mitochondrial functioning, resulting in better sleep. *Autophagy* is required for healthy brain cell mitochondria[xxviii]. Regular fasting does the trick as well, but regularly limiting your protein intake is another great way to do this. This makes your cells find every possible way to recycle proteins endogenously. At the same time, they bind and excrete toxins that are hidden in your cell's cytoplasm[xxix].

Being chronically protein deficient is horrible for the brain and body. The trick is to do it intermittently, like with fasting. After skipping protein intake completely (24-hour fast) or reducing your intake close to zero (about 15 grams), you'll supercompensate for that scarcity and increase its utilization. On a plant based vegan diet you don't have to worry that much about the negative side-effects of eating too much protein too often, but you can still benefit from abstaining from consuming it every once in a while.

Doing some form of intermittent fasting daily in concert with keto is one of the greatest health hacks there is. It doesn't even feel like an abstention if we structure it strategically. That's why the minimum fasting window I would recommend for everyone is 14-16 hours.

**Here's how to maximize your daily intermittent fasting and ketogenic eating.**

- Instead of having breakfast first thing in the morning, continue to fast for a few hours.

- Drink a lot of water to keep yourself hydrated. Either add some salt or drink mineral water.

- Wait until you get hungry and then drink either black coffee or tea.

- Fast for about 14-18 hours until noon. HGH and other hormones will have peaked by that time.

- Before you eat, have a glass of warm lemon water. The citric acid will promote the creation of good digestive enzymes and prepares your gut for digestion.

- Break your fast with something small. Eating a big meal will put too much stress on your intestines. Have a few nuts and vegetables with some fat. You shouldn't feel the need to eat more than 300-500 calories

- Wait a few hours and continue eating the rest of your calories.

To be honest, the majority of the benefits will be covered with that short time period. However, having a 24-hour fast once a week and a 48-hour one every few months will do your health an extraordinary service.

# Chapter VI

## A Definitive Guide to a Plant Based Keto Diet

And there you have it. You now know everything you need to know about the vegan keto diet. The standard ketogenic diet alone is very difficult and requires a lot of attention. This version is even more so.

However, once you get used to it, it will probably get easy. You simply have to go through the adaptation process and be mindful of how much carbs and protein you're consuming.

With the information you've received, you're already more knowledgeable than the majority of people. It's an essential and vital skill to know what effect food has on us and how to optimize it.

What we eat has a lot more profound impact on us than we think. High end performance and a good quality life require us to take care of our body.

The standard ketogenic diet alone is very difficult and requires a lot of attention. This version is even more so. However, once you get used to it, it will probably get easy. You simply have to go through the adaptation process and be mindful of how much carbs and protein you're consuming.

**It starts with the gut.** Our stomach is the closest point of contact we have with the world and is the most sensitive to external stimulus. What we put into our mouth will travel down our throat into the intestines where it will be used appropriately. If what you swallowed was food, hopefully, your body will release hydrochloric acid (HCA), which begins the digestion process.

Gut integrity and health is associated the most with bodily inflammation levels, which is the greatest predictor of overall health and longevity. Inhabited by millions of bacteria, our microbiome operates like a second brain that is constantly communicating with the rest of the body and sending out signals about what processes to conduct at any given moment.

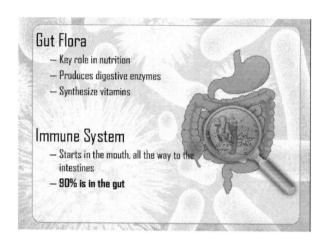

By being inflamed we will begin to suffer joint pain, brain fog and overall slothfulness. The 90% of our body's population is non-human and they control our appetite, hormones, metabolism and mood. It is essential to keep our gut clean and happy so that we too could feel great.

The reason why this is so important is that it will determine how well you're going to do on this ketogenic diet. If you neglect your gut, your brain and overall life will suffer.

## *It Starts with a Healthy Gut*

Dark leafy greens are excellent sources of fiber, vitamins, enzymes and minerals that feed the good gut microbiome.

Adding in excellent sources of fat and protein we are allowing our food to be digested properly and do it with ease without causing inflammation.

On the other hand, if we were to consume refined carbohydrates or whole grains then we will eventually get leaky gut, which is a syndrome where the phytates and gluten compounds destroy the intestinal walls, allowing the waste to flood our blood stream. As a result, we will suffer all of the diseases we are trying to avoid. Gluten-free might be considered a fad by some, but it's based on real science and physiology.

One thing to avoid entirely is the use of antibiotics. If you're taking some, then I advise you to find a better solution because these drugs kill all bacteria, the good and the bad. Also, you will cause gut irritation and excessive stress. Your body will heal itself from almost anything over time. Mostly our own behavior puts a halt to it. What we can do is assist the process.

Start eating an anti-inflammatory ketogenic diet. By removing processed food from your menu and eating plenty of healthy vegetables, fat and nuts, you're already solving the issue to a great degree.

In addition to that, eating fermented foods is a must. You should eat at least some form of it every day. As weird as it might sound, your plate has to be full of nutrition as well as crawling with bacteria. The best sources are sauerkraut, pickles, kimchi, tempeh, Kombucha, raw milk, raw yogurt and kefir. You can make all of them at home yourself. Commercial products aren't nearly as effective and can have added sugar in them.

**Here's how to make your own sauerkraut.**

**Ingredients**

- o Cabbage

- o An empty jar

- o Salt, pepper, or any other spices you like.

- o A food processor.

**Preparation**

- o Use the food processor to shred the cabbage.

- o Pack it tightly together with the spices into the jar.

- o The released liquid creates its own brining solution.

- o Leave the jar open and put a rock or something heavy on top of the cabbage for extra pressure.

- o Keep it at room temperature at somewhere with access to air.

- o After a few days, the cabbage will have fermented and is ready to be eaten.

## *What Changes You Should Make*

Start taking care of your gut, eat fermented foods and pay more attention to your overall inflammation levels. If you feel worse after eating something, then you probably shouldn't eat it again.

The ketogenic diet works so great because you'll be cleaning your body and resetting it back to its primal functioning. You'll learn more about how you react to different nutrients and how to optimize your intake accordingly. It's not worth it to feel anything less than great.

**Here are some additional changes we need to make to start a ketogenic lifestyle.**

- **Swap out your pantry.** Get rid of all of your whole grain breads, pastas, cereal, oatmeal, potatoes, fruit, sugar, rice etc. You don't need to have them in your house if you're not going to eat them. At least lose them for the time being. They can only hinder your process. If there are only keto foods around, then you won't even get the thought of wanting to eat carbohydrates. You begin to crave carbs only after you take a bite of them. Pre-empt that in advance like a strategic genius.

- **Buy a lot of healthy ketogenic food.** To replace the carbs, go to a supermarket and stack up on some staple nutrients that you'll be consuming from now on. It might seem like keto is overly restrictive but in reality there is quite a lot of variation in the diet. Some of the essential ingredients you should stock up on are.

- o <u>Extra Virgin Olive Oil</u>– Make sure you get it in a dark bottle. You don't want to expose it to sunlight or heat, as it will go rancid and cause oxidative damage. Don't use it on a frying pan either. Use it only as cold dressing.

- o <u>Extra Virgin Coconut Oil</u> – The best fat for cooking is coconut oil because its smoking point is 350°F/175°C. It's also full of medium-chain triglycerides, which are fatty acid chains with medium length bonds and can be quickly converted to energy.

- o **Frozen vegetables.** To get the most nutrients from your food, you should always try to eat it as fresh as possible. Moments after picking up a vegetable, the micronutrient content begins to diminish. However, refrigerating food will maintain its freshness, as it gets flash frozen right on the field. Buy a lot of frozen broccoli, cauliflower, kale, Brussels sprouts, green beans etc.

- **Stack up on healthy seasoning.**

- Pink Himalayan Rock Salt – Hydration and electrolyte balance are incredibly important on a ketogenic diet. By ditching carbs, your body will flush out a lot of liquids, which needs to be compensated by drinking more water and increasing your sodium intake. Ordinary table salt is contaminated with unhealthy nitrates. A good quality sea or pink salt also has a higher magnesium content, which is an essential nutrient to have.

- **Turmeric.** One of the best spices we can use is curcumin or turmeric. It has a lot of medicinal properties, such as anti-inflammatory compounds, increase of antioxidants and brain health. Also, it fights and prevents many diseases, such as Arthritis, Alzheimer's and even cancer. In addition to that, it tastes amazing and can be added to everything. I sprinkle it on all foods and run out quite quickly which is why I also buy it in bulk so that it's cheaper. You can also take a capsule.

- **Ginger.** Continuing on with turmeric's brother. It has almost as much health benefits. In addition to that, it lowers blood sugar levels, fights heart disease, treats chronic indigestion, may reduce menstrual pain for women, lowers cholesterol and heals muscle pain. Once again, <u>bulk</u> or <u>capsule</u>.

- o **Cinnamon.** These three create the most important natural spices we should be eating on a daily basis. They're incredibly cheap and easy to come by yet have amazing health as well as performance enhancing benefits. Moreover, they all make food taste amazing. Cinnamon falls into the same category as ginger and turmeric - superfoods, because it truly empowers us. In addition to the same medicinal properties it also increases insulin sensitivity, fights neurodegenerative disease and bacterial infections. What's best about it is that it can be added to not only salty foods but on desserts as well. I even add it to my coffee. The best to use is <u>Ceylon</u> or „true" cinnamon.

- **Calculate your macros.** You don't need to take this to neurotic levels. However, during the initial few weeks of adaptation, you should pay some attention to this. Weigh your food for a few days and follow the ketogenic macronutrient ratios.

- o **Carbs.** The total caloric proportion should be about 5-10% NET, which doesn't include the fiber. This will fall somewhere between 30-50 grams per day. Carb tolerances vary between individuals and you should know where yours lies. The lower your carb intake the faster will ketosis be induced. After the adaptation period you can get away with eating slightly more and don't have to worry about it that much.

- o **Protein.** The ketogenic diet is moderate in protein with 15-25% of total calories. If you're a sedentary person, then your demands will be even less. As a general guideline stick to somewhere between 0.7 to 1.3 grams per pound of lean body mass. If you're a hard-charging athlete, your needs will be higher.

- o **Fat.** The rest of your calories will come from fat, more than 70-80%. Eating more will not hurt your keto-adaptation. However, it's still a source of dense calories. If you're trying to lose weight, then you can't do so by eating at a surplus. You still have to be at a negative energy balance. The reason why keto works so great for this is that the satiety factor will by default make you eat less.

You can also use this free online macro calculator http://keto-calculator.ankerl.com/

### *Superfoods*

On the other hand, there are also some additional "superfoods" we can consume. They are slightly less conventional and harder to find. Nevertheless, they are incredibly empowering and take it to the next level. Occasionally using them will yield great results.

First off, it's important to understand what we mean by "superfoods." Broccoli and turmeric fight cancer and reduce inflammation, eggs and salmon have omega-3s and DHA and can be considered as such. Because of the benefits we get from them, they are already a part of the list. However, they lack that one last push that would twist the entire thing over the top.

A superfood for a superhuman would have to be something that transcends their health and performance past our normal capacities and reach levels of post-optimal wellbeing.

**Here's a list of some TRUE superfoods.**

- **Blueberries.** Why? They're full of phytonutrients, that neutralize free radicals (agents that cause aging and cell damage). High antioxidant content also protects against cancer and reduces the effects of Alzheimer's and Parkinson's disease. They're brain food that improves cognitive functioning and memory. At the same time, it reduces the risk of heart disease and muscle damage from exercise.

- **Cacao.** Not hot chocolate, but <u>raw cacao nibs</u>. They can improve your memory, reduce heart disease, increase fat oxidation, boost immunity and grant a lot of energy. The Incas considered it the drink of the gods. Raw cacao contains 20 times more antioxidants than blueberries and 119 times more than bananas. Processed chocolate is made with roasted cocoa, milk, sugar and trans fats that block the absorption of antioxidants. Organic more than 80% dark chocolate can have the same benefits as raw cacao.

- **Chia seeds.** A very popular superfood because of its nutrient density and easy digestion. Aztec warriors ate chia seeds before battle for high energy and endurance. A spoonful was said to sustain them for 24 hours. In the Mayan language, "Chia" means "strength." These seeds are rich in fiber, omega-3s, protein, vitamins and minerals, such as copper, zinc and potassium. They will boost our metabolism, protect against heart disease, build muscle and increase fat burning. To get the most nutrition out of them you have to soak them in water for a few hours before consumption.

- **Algae.** It's a complex superfood that can be found in green, blue-green or brown seaweed. The health benefits are quite amazing: stronger immune system, increased white blood cell count and better gut flora. Blue-green algae like Chlorella or Spirulina is a source of vitamin B12 and 22 other amino acids. Brown algae contains Fuxoaxanthin that promotes fat burning.

Start implementing these strategies here and you'll be living the ketogenic lifestyle. Buy good quality food, take care of your gut, change some of your eating habits and do intermittent fasting. You'll be off to achieving optimal health and wellbeing.

# *Chapter VII*

## *The Vegan Keto Cookbook*

I'm not going to lie... the list of foods is quite limited. However, that doesn't mean we can't make delicious meals. We simply have to use some imagination and follow a few recipes.

Here are some amazing low carb high fat vegan keto recipes you can eat on a daily basis.

### *Low Carb Vegan Bowls*

**Ingredients:**

- ¼ cup extra virgin olive oil
- ¼ cup lemon juice
- 1 tbsp poppy seeds
- 1 tsp powdered or grated ginger
- ¼ tsp sea salt
- 1 avocado
- 1 cup of grated cauliflower
- 2 tbsp of tahini

**Preparation:**

- Mix together the olive oil, lemon juice, poppy seeds, ginger and salt.
- Cut the avocado in half and remove the pit.
- Cover the cauliflower with the dressing.
- Add the dressing and tahini on the avocado.
- Enjoy as a small snack.

### *Vegan Keto Protein Salad*

**Ingredients:**

- ½ cup of Chia seeds
- ½ cup of Pumpkin seeds
- ¼ cup of olive oil
- 1 cup of mixed nuts of your choosing
- As much collard greens, lettuce you like
- ¼ cup of spinach
- ¼ tsp of salt and pepper

**Preparation:**

- Get a big bowl and put the vegetables inside.

- Add the seeds and oil, season according to preference.
- Get you protein in.

### *Chocolate Almond Butter Cookies*

**Ingredients:**

- ½ cup of almond or any other nut butter
- ¼ cup of coconut oil
- ¼ cup of cocoa powder
- 1/3 aquafaba or 1 vegan egg replacer
- 5 tbsp of Stevia
- 1 tsp of baking powder
- 1 tsp of vanilla extract

**Preparation:**

- Preheat the oven to 350 and put a baking sheet on your tray.
- Melt the coconut oil and mix it together with your nut butter and aquafaba/egg substitute.
- Add the vanilla, Stevia, baking powder and mix them together.
- Slowly stir in the cocoa and mix until nice and smooth.

- Put about tablespoon size portions on the tray and flatten them slightly. Leave about a few inches between each cookie, because they will spread once cooked.
- Put the tray in the oven for about 15 minutes until the edges get crispy. You'll know it once you see it.
- Let them cool for at least 15-20 minutes before trying to take them from the tray or they will crumble!
- Enjoy with some coconut milk. Just like in your childhood.

### *Chocolate Nut Butter Ice Cream*

**Ingredients:**

- 2-4 avocados
- ¼ cup cocoa powder
- ¼ cup of any nut butter
- 1 tbsp of Stevia
- 2 tbsp of coconut flakes
- 1 tbsp of cinnamon
- For additional crunch add some almonds, walnuts or pecans.

**Preparation:**

- Peel the avocados and put them into a blender or a food processor.
- Add cocoa and the butter and blend until smooth and creamy.
- Mix together with the coconut flakes and cinnamon. Add some nuts, if you want more crunch.
- Put the mixture into a tightly-sealed freezer-safe container.
- Freeze for about 3-4 hours.
- *Bon Appetite!*

## *Kale Chips*

**Ingredients:**

- Some sort of leafy fibrous greens. Kale, savoy cabbage, bok choy, collard greens etc.
- Seasoning according to preference.

**Preparation:**

- Wash the vegetables and cut the leaves into smaller pieces.

- Distribute them evenly on a pan and add seasoning.
- Don't add too much water into the bottom as it will make the greens too soft.
- Put the pan in the oven and bake for about 30-45 minutes on high heat.
- It's finished when the leaves will turn brown and crunchy.

## *Cauliflower Pizza*

The most amazing and versatile food at our disposal on keto is cauliflower. It can be used to substitute almost anything we're used to having: mashed potatoes, rice and pizza. This recipe will teach you how to have your gluten-free-low-carb crust that fits ketosis perfectly.

**Ingredients:**

- Cauliflower
- Egg substitute
- Tomatoes
- Seasoning and herbs of your choosing.

**Preparation:**

- Take the entire head of a cauliflower and cut off the florets.
- In a food processor shred them all into bits and pieces.
- Add in the egg substitute.
- Spread the mixture on a pan and put it in the oven for 30 minutes.
- This will turn into a crust and creates texture.
- Add the tomatoes on top and let it cook for a while until ready.

The same can be done with zucchini as well. Instead of it being pizza they look like boats instead. Simply cut the vegetable in half and add the other ingredients.

### *Avocado Mayonnaise*

**Ingredients:**

- Olive oil
- Lemon juice
- Avocados
- Mustard seeds

- Tabasco sauce
- Garlic cloves
- Salt and pepper

**Preparation:**

- Cut open the avocado and smash it down vigorously or use a blender.
- Add the seasoning and squeeze in the lemon juice.
- Crush the garlic cloves and mustard seeds and throw them in as well.
- A few drops of Tabasco for the extra burn.
- Slowly pour in the olive oil and keep mixing. Do it steadily and maintain a constant stream.
- Once it starts to thicken you know it's done.
- For more texture add more avocados or peanut butter.
- For more liquid add more oil.

The best way to make it is in bulk. Grab a jar and make a lot of it in advance. Store it in the freezer and use it as a sauce on your dishes. It tastes even better than the conventional mayonnaise and is completely keto-proof.

# *Vegan Keto Pancakes*

## Ingredients:

- Coconut milk
- Coconut oil
- Almond or coconut flour
- Egg substitute
- Cinnamon
- Blueberries and coconut flakes
- Optionally some vegan protein powder

## Preparation:

- Put the egg substitute into a mixing bowl.
- Pour in the coconut milk, protein powder and flour according to preference and texture.
- Mix them together with cinnamon.
- Heat the pan with coconut oil.
- Pour in the pancake mixture and cook on both sides.
- While in the pan throw some coconut flakes on top.
- Serve on a plate with blueberries.

As you can see there are many ways to eat a variety of delicious foods even with few ingredients. You can even enjoy meals from a normal diet plan. They taste as good and are a lot healthier. You simply have to use your imagination.

### *Coconut Keto Cereal*

If you've ever been a child (...), then you probably downed a lot of breakfast cereal. Tony the Tiger said its *"Grrreat!"* and our parents believed them. It has a lot of essential vitamins and minerals – everything a growing organism needs. But they're also filled with sugar, syrup, grains which make them not so great after all.

Yet again, we don't have to give up our crunchy cereal in the morning and can still eat keto. This recipe cooks the cereal in bulk. The actual serving size depends on how much you're going to eat.

- **Ingredients**
  - 1 whole package of <u>coconut flakes</u>
  - Cinnamon
  - <u>Stevia</u> (optional)

- Unsweetened almond milk
  - A few strawberries or blueberries
  - A handful of mixed nuts
  - 1 teaspoon of coconut oil
- **Preparation**
  - Preheat the oven to 350 F/180 C.
  - Grease a baking pan with coconut oil or use baking parchment instead.
  - Pour the coconut flakes on the pan and cook them for about 5 minutes. Keep watch the whole time.
  - Shuffle the flakes and stir them around. Keep cooking until they're slightly tan and toasted.
  - Take the flakes out and sprinkle with cinnamon.
  - To eat, take about ½ cups of the chips and put them into a bowl. Pour in the almond milk, slice in the berries and add a few more nuts.
  - Bon appetite!

### *Keto Spaghetti Squash*

Another Italian classic that doesn't require wheat or whole grains.

- **Ingredients**
  - 1 spaghetti squash
  - 2 tablespoons of butter
  - 1/4 cup of heavy cream or coconut milk
  - Salt and pepper
  - ½ cups of grated cheese
  - A pinch of basil
- **Preparation**
  - Preheat the oven to 375 F/180 C
  - Slice the squash in half, lengthwise, and remove the seeds and pulp.
  - Wrap both halves in aluminum foil, place them face-up on a baking sheet and bake for about 30-40 minutes.
  - Once done, scoop out the flesh with a fork, which will create these spaghetti like figures.
  - Melt the butter over medium heat and add the heavy cream, salt, cheese and basil. Cook for about 10-15 minutes at a light simmer, while stirring every once in a while.
  - Add the spaghetti squash, mix and enjoy!

## *Cucumber Spinach Smoothie*

An effortless way to get in more greens into your diet is to juice them. You can use many variations of this same recipe, using different ingredients.

- **Ingredients**
  - 2 handfuls of spinach
  - 1 large cucumber
  - 7 ice cubes
  - 1/2 cups of coconut milk
  - 1 teaspoon of Stevia
- **Preparation**
  - Cut the cucumber into slices or cubes.
  - Throw in all of the ingredients into a blender and blend.
  - Absorb all of the vitamins and minerals of greens.

## *Cauli Hash*

- **Ingredients**
  - 2 tablespoons of coconut oil
  - ½ onion, chopped
  - 2-4 garlic cloves, minced
  - About 1 pound of cauliflower steamed and chopped into small chunks.
  - Turmeric, ginger, salt and pepper

- o ½ green bell peppers
- **Preparation**
    - o Sautee the onions in butter for a few minutes over medium heat.
    - o After 5 minutes, add the garlic and bell pepper
    - o Squeeze all excess water from your steamed cauliflower. Add it to the pan and sautee for 5-10 minutes until brown and crispy.
    - o Add the seasoning and toss all of the ingredients around for another 2 minutes.
    - o Throw the mix into a bowl and have a nice meal!

## ***Pan Fried Avocado***

If you don't have a lot of time or aren't that hungry, you can easily have a simple yet tasty small little meal.

- **Ingredients**
    - o 1 avocado
    - o 2 tablespoons of <u>coconut oil</u>
    - o Sea salt
- **Preparation**
    - o Cut avocado in half and remove the pit.
    - o Peel and cut into small cubes.
    - o Melt the coconut oil over medium heat.

- Add the avocado and cook for a few minutes until only slightly brown. Stir occasionally. Don't overdo with the heat, as fats will go rancid.
- Season with salt and *voila!*

### *Coconut Cream Porridge*

It's thought that oatmeal is incredibly healthy. Well, it might be, but it's definitely not optimal because of gluten and the phytates found in whole grains.

Nevertheless, there's still a way to have a bowl of keto porridge that tastes equally as good and doesn't come with any negative effects.

- **Ingredients**
  - 1 cup of coconut cream
  - 1 oz of almonds (about 20), ground or whole
  - 1 teaspoon of cinnamon and Stevia (optional)
  - 1 teaspoon of coconut flakes
  - A pinch of nutmeg
- **Preparation**
  - Heat the coconut cream on a saucepan on medium until it forms a liquid.
  - Add the almonds, coconut flakes and stevia
  - Mix well and keep stirring for a few minutes until it begins to thicken.

- Add the cinnamon, nutmeg and taste.
- Serve hot.

## *Blueberry Popsicles*

More ice cream. This time it's popsicles.

- **Ingredients**
    - 100g of blueberries
    - 1 lemon cut in half
    - 1 cup of coconut milk or almond milk
    - 1 teaspoon of Stevia
- **Preparation**
    - Add the ingredients into a container and blend the mixture together.
    - Continue blending until the blueberries are completely mixed in with all of the ingredients.
    - Pour the mixture into popsicle molds and put them in the freezer for a minimum of 2 hours.
    - Take out the molds and run them under hot water to dislodge the popsicles.
    - Enjoy your little treat!

As you can see there are many ways to eat a variety of delicious foods even with few ingredients. You can even enjoy meals from a normal diet plan. They taste as good and are a lot healthier. You simply have to use your imagination.

# Chapter VIII

## Vegan Keto Supplements

Despite our access to abundant contemporary food we're still missing some key ingredients - the micronutrients. To overcome this flaw there are some supplements we should be taking.

Health is not something to be taken for granted and being superhuman requires doing what's necessary for achieving that status. What matters more about any type of food is not its caloric proportions but the minerals, enzymes, vitamins etc. and what hormonal effect it has on the organism.

With the industrialization of food all of that has suffered. Our soils are being depleted from their vital life force with the use of fertilizers, spraying of toxic fumes, usage of GMOs, radiation, travel pollution and many other things. All for the purpose of creating more empty calories and food without any actually beneficial content.

As a vegan supplementation is even more important because it's difficult to get all of the essential amino acids and fatty acids from solely plant based food.

A word of caution. There are a lot of supplements we could be taking. However, that doesn't mean we should start gorging on piles of tablets and numerous pills. It's not about becoming a substance junkie, but a self-empowered being who simply covers all of the necessary micronutrients through the usage of natural yet still manufactured additives.

**We don't need to take a whole lot, simply some which everyone needs and especially those that we're individually most deficient of.** That's something we have to find out ourselves.

We don't need to fear these pharmaceuticals just because their artificial form. They are just natural ingredients that have been processed and put into a bottle or a powder.

All of the supplements that I have listed here are least processed and free from any additional garbage, such as preservatives, GMO, gluten, starch, sugar etc. They're keto-proof and vegan friendly.

**Additionally, we should always try to stick to real whole foods as much as possible.** Supplements are just that - supplementation for some of the deficiencies we fail to get from what we actually eat. They're not magical but simply give us the extra edge.

The effects these products have can be derived from natural foods as well. In the form of a pill or a powder they're simply microscopic and packaged nutrition. Taking them will grant us access to optimal health - the utmost level of wellbeing and performance both physical and mental.

In this list are all of the supplements I am personally taking because of their importance, as well as the additional benefits we get. However, I do not advise anyone to take any of them unless they are aware of their medical condition and don't know about the possible side effects or issues that may or may not follow.

**Before taking anything we ought to educate ourselves about the topic and consult a professional physician. <u>The responsibility is solely on the individual and I will take none.</u>**

## Natural Seasoning

To start off I'm going to list the supplements we should be taking, each and every one of us. I already discussed the importance of using turmeric, ginger and cinnamon every day. In case you forgot, here they are again.

- **Turmeric.** One of the best spices we can use is curcumin or turmeric. It has a lot of medicinal properties, such as anti-inflammatory compounds, increase of antioxidants and brain health. Also, it fights and prevents many diseases, such as Arthritis, Alzheimer's and even cancer. In addition to that, it tastes amazing and can be added to everything. I sprinkle it on all foods and run out quite quickly which is why I also buy it in <u>bulk</u> so that it's cheaper. You can also take a <u>capsule</u>.

- **Ginger.** Continuing on with turmeric's brother. It has almost as much health benefits. In addition to that, it lowers blood sugar levels, fights heart disease, treats chronic indigestion, may reduce menstrual pain for women, lowers cholesterol and heals muscle pain. Once again, <u>bulk</u> or <u>capsule</u>.

- **Cinnamon.** These three create the most important natural spices we should be eating on a daily basis. They're incredibly cheap and easy to come by yet have amazing health as well as performance enhancing benefits. Moreover, they all make food taste amazing. Cinnamon falls into the same category as ginger and turmeric - superfoods, because it truly empowers us. In addition to the same medicinal properties it also increases insulin sensitivity, fights neurodegenerative disease and bacterial infections. What's best about it is that it can be added to not only salty foods but on desserts as well. I even add it to my coffee. The best to use is Ceylon or „true" cinnamon.

- **Green tea.** It isn't an actual supplement but is still extremely empowering. In fact, it can be considered to be the healthiest beverage of the world after water. It improves health, brain function, fat oxidation and detoxifies the system. Additionally, lowers blood pressure and prevents all types of disease, including Alzheimer's and cancer. We don't need to take pills with extracts but can get all of the benefits by simply drinking a cup a day.

However, to get all of the benefits we need to be consuming about 15-30 cups. Using a <u>capsule</u> would be very efficient.

- **Garlic.** It has a strong taste and smell but is incredibly healthy nonetheless. Chopping garlic cloves forms a compound called allicin, which, once digested, travels all over the body and exerts its potent biological effects. It fights all illness, especially the cold, reduces blood pressure, improves cholesterol levels, contains antioxidants, increases longevity, detoxifies the body from metals, promotes bone health and is delicious. Because of its flavor it makes a great addition to meals. It also comes in <u>capsuled</u> form.

### *Supplements you HAVE to Take*

Moving on with actual supplements. These things we're all deficient of and they also take our performance to the next level, they empower us.

- **Omega-3s** are great for the brain and heart. The counterpart to that is omega-6, which are pro-inflammatory and bad for us. Omega-6 can be found in a lot of processed foods and vegetable oils, which we would want to avoid anyway. For our body to be healthy the omega-3's need to be in balance with the omega-6's. Unfortunately, that balance can be easily tipped off as every amount of omega-6 requires triple the amount of omega-3 to reduce the negative effects. Additionally, DHA and EPA, promote brain functioning, fight inflammation, support bone health, increase physical performance etc. Naturally, they can be found in fatty fish such as salmon, herring, mackerel and sardines. Chia seeds have some as well, but as a vegan you HAVE to supplement this. There are some <u>softgels</u> you can easily take.

- **Vitamin D-3.** This is the sunshine vitamin and is one of the most important nutrients. Life exists on Earth because of the Sun. D-3 governs almost every function within us starting from DNA repair and metabolic processes making it a foundation to everything that goes on. It's embedded in nutritious food, given it has received enough exposure to solar light. Vitamin D-3 fights cardiovascular, autoimmune and infective diseases. Of course, the best source would be to get it from the Sun but that is not always possible because of seasonality and location. It can be consumed as <u>oil</u> or a <u>capsule</u>.

- **Magnesium.** Another foundational mineral. It comprises 99% of the body's mineral content and governs almost all of the processes. Magnesium helps to build bones, enables nerves to function and is essential for the production of energy from food. This is especially beneficial for the physically active. Some people who are depressed get headaches because of this deficiency. Because our soils are quite depleted magnesium needs to be <u>supplemented</u>. It can also be used as an <u>oil</u> on your skin for greater absorption in specific areas.

- **Vitamin B-12**. It's a water soluble vitamin with key properties for normal brain and nervous system functioning. You need it for the formulation of red blood cells as well. Starting with DNA synthesis and ending with amino acid metabolism, it's involved with every cell in the body. We aren't capable of producing it and therefore need to derive it from diet. The best sources of B-12 are animal products and that's why vegans tend to suffer a deficiency from this vital vitamin. Eating unwashed organic vegetables is a popular way to circumvent that, but it's not enough. You also have to <u>supplement</u> it.

### ***Supplements Empowered***

We have covered all of the supplements you should be taking as a low carb vegan no matter what, the most important and essential ones. Now I'll get down to the empowering ones.

They are not foundational but beneficial nonetheless. With the help of these we can transcend the boundary between healthy and superhuman performance as they will take us to the next level.

- **Creatine Monohydrate.** Creatine is an organic acid produced in the liver that helps to supply energy to cells all over the body, especially muscles. It enhances ATP production and allows for muscle fibers to contract faster, quicker, and makes them overall stronger. That means

134

increased physical performance with explosive and strength based movements and sprinting. However, it doesn't end there. Creatine has been found to improve cognitive functioning, as it's a nootropic as well, improving mental acuity and memory. Naturally, it can be found most in red meat. It's <u>dirty cheap</u> and easy to consume, as only 5 grams per day will do wonders and doing so won't make a person big nor bulky.

- **Pro- and prebiotics.** Having a well working digestive system is incredibly vital for getting the most nutrients out of our food. Industrialization has done another disservice to us by destroying all of the bacteria in the food we consume, the good and the bad, and replacing them with preservatives. We might be eating but we're not actually deriving a lot of nutrients. In order to have a healthy gut we need to have a well-functioning microbiome. Naturally, food is full of living organisms. Sauerkraut, raw milk, yoghurt, unprocessed meat all have good bacteria in them. With there being no life in our food, we need to create it within us ourselves. <u>Probiotics</u> are alive microorganisms in a pill that transport these good bacteria into our gut for improved digestion and immune system. Prebiotics are different, they're not alive, but plant fiber that feeds the bacteria. They're indigestible parts of the vegetable that go through our digestive track into our gut where the bacteria then eat them. If you don't like eating a lot of broccoli and spinach, then you should still get a lot of fiber into your diet.

- **Thyroid supplementation.** The thyroid gland is incredibly important for our health because it regulates the functioning of our metabolism. Moreover, because of its location in our throat it also is a connective point between the brain and the rest of the body. This organ is a part of an incredibly complex system which creates this intertwined relationship between the two. With a low functioning thyroid one will have an impeded metabolism, suffer hypothyroidism and many other diseases because of the necessary hormones will not be produced. Promoting thyroid functioning can be done by taking iodine supplementation or eating a lot of sea vegetables. The daily requirements for selenium can be met with eating only 2-3 Brazil nuts.

- **Multivitamin.** There are definitely a lot of vitamins to be covered for our body to not only be healthy but function at its peak. It would be unreasonable to take too many tablets or pills while neglecting the importance of real food. However, taking a multivitamin that has a lot of beneficial minerals all combined into one <u>bottle</u> is very effective and will most definitely be useful.

- **Maca.** Another superfood comes from the Peruvian mountains and is the root of ginseng. It has numerous amounts of vitamins and minerals in it, such as magnesium zinc, copper etc. Also, it promotes hormone functioning for both men and women, as well as increases our energy production just like creatine does. It can either be <u>powdered</u> or made into a <u>tablet</u>.

- **GABA.** Called gamma-aminobutyric acid, it's the main inhibitory neurotransmitter, and regulates the nerve impulses in the human body. Therefore, it is important for both physical and mental performance, as both of them are connected to the nervous system. Also, <u>GABA</u> is to an extent responsible for causing relaxation and calmness, helping to produce BDNF.

- **Chaga mushroom.** Chaga is a mushroom that grows on birch trees. It's extremely beneficial for supporting the immune system, has anti-oxidative and soothing properties, lowers blood pressure and cholesterol. Also, consuming it will promote the health and integrity of the adrenal glands. This <u>powder</u> can be added to teas or other warm beverages. Or you can <u>grind it yourself</u>.

- **MCT oil.** For nutritional ketosis having an additional source of ketone bodies will be beneficial. MCT stands for medium chain triglycerides which are fat molecules that can be digested more rapidly than normal fat ones, which are usually long chain triglycerides. Doing so will enable the brain to have immediate access to abundant energy and a deeper state of ketosis. Basically, it's glucose riding the vessel of ketones. Naturally, it's extracted from <u>coconut oil</u> and is an enhanced liquidized version of it. Additionally, I also eat raw <u>coconut flakes</u>, which have <u>MCTs</u> in them.

- **Branched Chain Amino Acids.** L-Leucine, L-Isoleucine, and L-Valine are grouped together and called BCAAs because of their unique chemical structure. They're essential and have to be derived from diet. Supplementing them will increase performance, muscle recovery and protein synthesis. There is no solid evidence to show any significant benefit to BCAAs. However, they can be very useful <u>to take</u> before fasted workouts to reduce muscle catabolism. As a vegan you can also take them to cover all of your essential amino acids.

This is the list of supplements we should be taking. It includes the most important ones, the essential, which we should be taking no matter what, as well as the not so vital that simply make us more empowered and give us the extra edge. Nothing replaces good food, but proper and educated supplementation will fix some of the loopholes.

# Bonus Chapter

## How to Get into Ketosis at Lightning Speed

Before you start living the ketogenic lifestyle, you may want to speed up your adaptation process. This chapter teaches you how to get into nutritional ketosis super fast.

To get into ketosis we have to either:

- Fast for a prolonged amount of time.

- Restrict our carbohydrate intake to a bare minimum.

Both options are very effective ways of inducing ketosis.

However, those two things aren't always enough. **Someone who is burning sugar may not ever be able to get into ketosis, despite following the guidelines.** The body is just too addicted to sugar and enters an energy crisis.

To provide energy for the brain and body, it is necessary to have a substitute for glucose. If you want to become fat adapted, then you have to promote the production of ketone bodies as well. To do that, we would have to consume fat that is easily absorbed and gives quick energy.

**The #1 source of quality fat is probably MCT oil.** There are also exogenous ketones but at the moment they are not that commercially available. For habitual use, MCTs get the job done and are great.

To promote ketone production, we can eat any other type of fat as well. Coconut oil, avocado oil and olive oil are only slightly less effective.

### *How to Get Into Ketosis Fast*

Fasting is the most natural and effective ways of inducing ketosis. After a few days the body will be utilizing primarily fat for fuel because there is no glucose left to be found. In addition to that, it will derive energy solely from the adipose tissue.

To not become excessively gluconeogenic and begin to cannibalize your precious muscles and organs, then you need to provide yourself with at least some form of energy.

**Consuming only fat, with no other macronutrient will not even put you into a fed state.** The calories will not cross the blood-brain barrier and it actually mimicks fasting. Because your blood sugar levels will not be affected, you will continue to fast. The exception is that now you will have higher ketone levels and increased energy.

**This is called fat fasting.** It takes the 2 best ways of getting into ketosis and makes the adaptation process even faster.

Doing this will not be very taxing to the body. For a sugar burner it will definitely be quite difficult. Lowering their carbohydrate intake even just a little bit will cause withdrawal symptoms. What would you expect from a full on ban then?

For someone who already knows how to use fat for fuel, this will be actually quite enjoyable. It will feel like fasting but you'll have a lot of energy. After a few days, you should be in quite deep ketosis.

**But how much fat should you consume?** There isn't any upper or lower limit, really. However, there will definitely be <u>a point of diminishing returns</u>. Once that threshold has been crossed, you won't get any extra benefit from consuming more MCTs. You'll simply be eating calories.

It's better to keep your fat intake as low as possible and use it only when necessary. To not exit your fasted state, you would only want to take one teaspoon a few times a day. This would total under 500 calories that are all derived from fat.

### *Mistakes to Avoid*

Fat fasting is a great way to get into ketosis faster, but it shouldn't be taken too far. During the adaptation phase, you'll be still quite catabolic and dependent of glucose.

You're still going to have to go through several days of adaptation before you make a complete shift. But you don't want to be fasting for that long.

If you're obese or sedentary, then you can get away with it easily. If you're physically active and a fit individual, then you shouldn't fast for that long. In that case, you would want to do it for a day or two on days when you're not training. This should only be a strategy to kick-start the process.

Also, you wouldn't want to neglect the principles of ketogenic dieting. This is not a quick fix, but simply a very time-efficient strategy. Don't think that this will put you into deep ketosis for the rest of your life. After breaking the fast you would still want to continue eating low carb, to stay adapted.

# Conclusion

## *Plant Based High Fat Low Carb – What's Next?*

To be honest, I was skeptical myself when I first started researching this. You don't really hear the words *"vegan"* and *"keto"* in one sentence, not to mention a diet program. Unless, of course they're bashing each other.

But what this book and some people have proven is that it's possible to eat a low carb high fat plant based diet. It's possible to get into ketosis and stay in it.

This is such a new and innovative way of eating that giving any long term judgements isn't yet possible. That's why I encourage you to try it out. You can become the pathfinder of a movement.

Like I said in the beginning, I'm not a vegan but simply a keto expert. To be honest, I don't think a vegan ketogenic diet would be sustainable for me because of my athletic pursuits. However, it can potentially work for you if you're less active. Also, getting the majority of my protein from meat substitutes and soy wouldn't be ideal for my health. But who knows where science will lead us next? Maybe we'll soon get access to food that puts us into ketosis and makes us Superhuman without us having to kill sentient beings.

Until then, if you want to learn more about keto and join the "dark side", then you can check out some of my other books. They're about different variations of the ketogenic diet and can work miracles for you.

That's why I'm going to share with you <u>a concept of mine called optimal nutrition</u>. It can be grasped under a single sentence, which goes as follows:

**Optimal nutrition is eating the right things, in the right amounts at the right time.**

I do not know about you but I think there cannot be made a better definition than that. It covers all of what we need to know OBJECTIVELY, meaning that it is not taken out of context and can be applied to any situation. We simply need to decipher it and make it fit our demands.

Keto is a part of that, but it may not fit into the paradigm of optimal nutrition all of the time. For the most part it does. Even

I, who trains quite hard and often, feel this way. My body is very insulin sensitive but I still prefer to use fat for fuel.

On this note I'm going to end the book. Simple keto, right?

Before that, I also wanted to give you another FREE gift.

It's a short little e-book about the definition of optimal nutrition, in which I also decipher the whole concept into its smaller parts. You'll love it. It would be the next natural step to take on your nutritional journey.

## *FREE GIFT*

Click the image above or the link below to get the **FREE** e-book

called **Optimal Nutrition Report**..

Or if you're on the paperback version, head over to

http://siimland.com/optimal-nutrition-report

## Ultimate Keto Meal Plan

I've also created a 21 day ketogenic meal plan called Ultimate Keto, which will put ultimately into ketosis. It will help you to start a well-formulated ketogenic diet as a long term thing. Check it out at http://siimland.com/ultimate-keto-meal-plan/

Click here to get Ultimate Keto!

## *More Books from the Author*

Read more books in my Simple Keto series. They're more advanced protocols of the ketogenic diet and used to maximize athletic performance while eating low carb.

Find out how to workout on keto and build muscle from the book Keto Bodybuilding

Keto Bodybuilding: Build Lean Muscle and Burn Fat at the Same Time by Eating a Low Carb Ketogenic Bodybuilding Diet and Get the Physique of a Greek God

Keto Cycle the Cyclical Ketogenic Diet Book

Simple Keto the Easiest Ketogenic Diet Book

## Target Keto the Targeted Ketogenic Diet Book

## Optimal Nutrition Program: Eat to Become Superhuman

## Intermittent Fasting and Feasting: Use Strategic Periods of Undereating and Overfeeding to Unleash the Most Powerful Anabolic Hormones of Your Body

Also, other books of mine.

<u>Becoming a Self Empowered Being</u>

# *About the Author*

Hello, my name is Siim Land and I'm a holistic health practitioner, a fitness expert, an author and a self-empowered being. Ever since my childhood I've been engaged with personal development and self-actualization. As a kid, I made the decision of improving the state of mankind and transcending humanity towards the better. My journey has lead me on an Odyssey of body-mind-spirit, during which I've managed to develop and enhance every aspect of my being. My philosophy is based around achieving self-mastery and excellence first and foremost. What comes after that is the mission of empowering others to do the same. That's what I've dedicated my life to and am doing daily. To do that, I'm always trying to improve upon my own physiology, psychology and biology. I dream of a better world, in which mankind isn't separated from one another and is working towards reaching their truest potential.

Contact me at my blog: http://siimland.com/contact

# *References*

Here are the links to the academic journals and scientific studies used in this book. If you're on the paperback version, then you can simply Google them and get the same results.

[i] Body composition and hormonal responses to a carbohydrate-restricted diet.

[ii] A high-fat, ketogenic diet induces a unique metabolic state in mice.

[iii] What is an Essential Nutrient?

[iv] Endocrine Notes on Glucose Metabolism (PDF)

[v] Glycerol gluconeogenesis in fasting humans.

[vi] Low-carbohydrate nutrition and metabolism

[vii] The Expensive-Tissue Hypothesis: The Brain and the Digestive System in Human and Primate Evolution

[viii] The Effects of a Ketogenic Diet on Exercise Metabolism and Physical Performance in Off-Road Cyclists

[ix] Nonenzymatic glucosylation and glucose-dependent cross-linking of protein.

[x] The AGE-receptor in the pathogenesis of diabetic complications.

[xi] Advanced glycation end products Key Players in Skin Aging?

[xii] The effects of a low-carbohydrate ketogenic diet and a low-fat diet on mood, hunger, and other self-reported symptoms.

[xiii] The National Cholesterol Education Program Diet vs a Diet Lower in Carbohydrates and Higher in Protein and Monounsaturated Fat

[xiv] HDL-subpopulation patterns in response to reductions in dietary total and saturated fat intakes in healthy subjects

[xv] Short-term effects of severe dietary carbohydrate-restriction advice in Type 2 diabetes--a randomized controlled trial.

[xvi] A low-carbohydrate, ketogenic diet to treat type 2 diabetes

[xvii] Metabolic syndrome and low-carbohydrate ketogenic diets in the medical school biochemistry curriculum

[xviii] Metabolic characteristics of keto-adapted ultra-endurance runners

[xix] Ketogenic diet does not affect strength performance in elite artistic gymnasts

[xx] Grimm O. Addicted to food. Scientific American Mind 2007; 18(2):36-39

[xxi] Nutrition and Physical Degeneration

[xxii] Liver and kidney metabolism during prolonged starvation

[xxiii] Short-term fasting induces profound neuronal autophagy

[xxiv] Enhanced thermogenic response to epinephrine after 48-h starvation in humans.

[xxv] Alternate-day fasting in nonobese subjects: effects on body weight, body composition, and energy metabolism.

[xxvi] Fasting enhances growth hormone secretion and amplifies the complex rhythms of growth hormone secretion in man.

[xxvii] Autophagy is required to maintain muscle mass.

[xxviii] Inflammation-Induced Alteration of Astrocyte Mitochondrial Dynamics Requires Autophagy for Mitochondrial Network Maintenance

[xxix] Autophagy in the Pathogenesis of Disease

Made in the USA
San Bernardino, CA
16 February 2017